understanding **utilitarianism**

Understanding Movements in Modern Thought
Series Editor: Jack Reynolds

This series provides short, accessible and lively introductions to the major schools, movements and traditions in philosophy and the history of ideas since the beginning of the Enlightenment. All books in the series are written for undergraduates meeting the subject for the first time.

Published

Understanding Empiricism
Robert G. Meyers

Understanding Existentialism
Jack Reynolds

Understanding Hegelianism
Robert Sinnerbrink

Understanding Hermeneutics
Lawrence K. Schmidt

Understanding Phenomenology
David R. Cerbone

Understanding Poststructuralism
James Williams

Understanding Utilitarianism
Tim Mulgan

Understanding Virtue Ethics
Stan van Hooft

Forthcoming titles include

Understanding Ethics
Tim Chappell

Understanding Feminism
Peta Bowden and Jane Mummery

Understanding German Idealism
Will Dudley

Understanding Naturalism
Jack Ritchie

Understanding Pragmatism
Axel Mueller

Understanding Psychoanalysis
Joanne Faulkner
and Matthew Sharpe

Understanding Rationalism
Charlie Heunemann

understanding **utilitarianism**

Tim Mulgan

ACUMEN

First published in 2007 by Acumen

Acumen Publishing Limited
Stocksfield Hall
Stocksfield
NE43 7TN
www.acumenpublishing.co.uk

ISBN: 978-1-84465-089-7 (hardcover)
ISBN: 978-1-84465-090-3 (paperback)

British Library Cataloguing-in-Publication Data
A catalogue record for this book is available from the British Library.

Typeset by Graphicraft Limited, Hong Kong.
Printed and bound by Cromwell Press, Trowbridge.

Contents

one

Introduction

What is utilitarianism?

In his brief essay *Utilitarianism*, John Stuart Mill provides a very succinct account of the Utility Principle.

> Actions are right in proportion as they tend to promote happiness, wrong as they tend to produce the reverse of happiness. By happiness is intended pleasure, and the absence of pain; by unhappiness, pain, and the privation of pleasure.
>
> (Mill, *Utilitarianism*, 55)

However, this deceptively simple principle is not the whole story. Utilitarianism is a broad tradition of philosophical and social thought, not a single principle. The central utilitarian idea is that morality and politics are (and should be) centrally concerned with the promotion of happiness. While Mill's principle is one expression of this basic idea, there are many others. In particular, Mill's principle focuses our attention on particular actions. As we shall see, utilitarians have often been more interested in evaluating codes of moral rules or systems of political institutions.

Why study utilitarianism?

If you are taking an introductory ethics course, then you will probably be asked questions about utilitarianism. If you want to pass the course, this gives you a reason to study utilitarianism. Fortunately, there are other – nobler – reasons to study utilitarianism. Throughout the past two centuries, the utilitarian tradition has been very influential – not just within philosophy, but in the more obviously practical disciplines of politics and economics. As a result of this influence, utilitarian assumptions and arguments abound in modern economic and political life, especially in public policy. If we want to understand the social world we inhabit, an understanding of the utilitarian tradition is essential.

In introductory ethics courses, utilitarianism is often presented as a deeply counter-intuitive theory – one which some philosophers accept despite its lack of intuitive appeal. As we shall see in Chapter 5, there are good reasons for this. Utilitarianism can face very severe intuitive problems. However, the central utilitarian idea also has considerable intuitive appeal. What could be more obvious than the thought that, in both our daily lives and our political deliberations, we should strive to make people's lives go better? What else should we want – to make people miserable?

Negative reactions to utilitarianism are often based on misunderstandings. Jeremy Bentham gave utilitarianism a bad name. And he knew it. Although Bentham sometimes used the name "principle of utility", he preferred the longer but more accurate "greatest happiness principle". The focus on "utility" suggests a dour, serious view, opposed to frivolity or fun. In everyday English, to describe a building as "utilitarian" is to say that it is merely functional. It gets the job done, but gives no one any pleasure or enjoyment. Sometimes utilitarians have encouraged this misunderstanding. But, properly understood, the utilitarian tradition points in the opposite direction. Pleasure, enjoyment and fun are all components of happiness. So they are all things that utilitarians want to promote. (Indeed, as we shall see in Chapter 4, utilitarian philosophers are often accused of being *too* interested in pleasure.)

Plan of the book

Introductions to utilitarianism typically take one of two forms. Some discuss the classical utilitarians from a purely *historical* perspective, without attempting to connect their work with subsequent developments in moral philosophy. At the other extreme, problem-based ethics courses are often entirely *ahistorical*, so that utilitarianism is presented as an abstract moral principle that miraculously emerged from the philosophical ether. My approach lies between these two extremes. I aim to present utilitarianism as a living tradition, as opposed to either an outdated view of merely historical interest or an ahistorical set of abstract principles.

Chapter 2 offers a brief history of the utilitarian tradition, showing how shifts in historical context have changed the priorities of utilitarian thinkers. We begin with a brief account of the precursors of classical utilitarianism, contrasting the conservative theological utilitarianism of William Paley with the radical atheism of William Godwin. The bulk of the chapter explores the evolution of classical utilitarianism from Bentham through J. S. Mill to Henry Sidgwick. The aim of the chapter is to illustrate both the current relevance of the classical utilitarians, and the extent to which their concerns differ from our own.

Over the past two hundred years, utilitarian thinkers have offered many justifications for their views. These are explored in Chapter 3. One central theme is that the style of these "proofs" has often been driven more by the prevailing philosophical orthodoxy of the time than by any internal debate within the utilitarian tradition. As a result, the chapter proceeds chronologically. It also includes potted summaries of broader developments in English language philosophy over the past two hundred years, from the early work of Bentham, through Mill's empiricism, the philosophical intuitionism of Sidgwick, and the mid-twentieth-century obsession with the analysis of moral language; to recent attempts to vindicate utilitarianism using the various methods of contemporary philosophy. (The broader philosophical history here deserves several books of its own. So my aim is merely to give a taste of the relationship between moral philosophy and broader philosophical trends. Other books in the Acumen *Understanding Movements in Modern Thought* series provide more detail on specific movements in modern philosophy.) We close by asking how these changes in underlying philosophical emphasis have affected the *content* of utilitarian morality. I argue that the shift away from attempts to construct deductive proofs of the utilitarian principle has increased the importance of the alleged counterintuitive consequences of the utilitarian principle. This paves the way for subsequent chapters.

Perhaps the most important question dividing utilitarians is the definition of happiness or "well-being" or "utility" or "whatever makes life worth living". (The fact the utilitarians use all these different terms – and more besides – is an indication of the complexities involved.)

Chapter 4 follows the debate from the classical utilitarians through to contemporary thinkers. We focus on three main alternatives: *hedonism* (a good life consists of pleasure), *preference theory* (a good life consists of getting what you want), and *objective list theory* (a good life consists of various things that are valuable in their own right, such as knowledge or achievement). Although historical material is introduced where relevant, our main interest is in the positions themselves, not on the thinkers who first propounded them.

Chapter 4 also introduces us to the methods of modern moral philosophy, especially the use of "thought experiments" to test a moral theory. The chapter ends with a discussion of the moral significance of the welfare of animals, and its connection to the well-being of humans. This issue is interesting in its own right, but it is also an excellent way to illustrate the differences between competing theories of *human* well-being.

Introductory ethics courses often begin with the "implausible" consequences of utilitarianism. Here are two classic examples.

The sheriff

You are the sheriff in an isolated wild-west town. A murder has been committed. Most people believe that Bob is guilty, but you know he is innocent. Unless you hang Bob now, there will be a riot in town and several people will die. Utilitarianism says you must hang Bob, because the loss of his life is outweighed by the value of preventing the riot.

The envelope

On your desk is an envelope addressed to a reputable charity seeking donations to save the lives of victims of a famine or other natural disaster. Utilitarianism says you should give *all* your money to this charity, as each dollar will produce more happiness in their hands than you could possibly produce by spending it on yourself.

Opponents argue that utilitarianism requires you to do something that is either clearly wrong (in the sheriff case) or clearly not obligatory (in the envelope case). Chapter 5 explores these objections. We begin by setting out a whole array of other alleged counter-examples, and asking what they have in common. We focus on a suggestion of John Rawls – utilitarianism's main fault is that, because it focuses on aggregate utility, it ignores or undervalues the *separateness of persons*. We then explore a range of utilitarian replies. This leads us to examine the role of *intuitions* in moral philosophy, following on from our discussion of the method of reflective equilibrium in Chapter 3. Why does it matter if utilitarianism has intuitively undesirable consequences? The chapter ends by noting that this cluster of objections does not seem to have worried classical utilitarians – especially Bentham and Mill. Perhaps the answer is to return to classical utilitarianism.

Chapter 6 asks if utilitarians can make their theory more intuitively appealing by changing its *scope*. Should utilitarians be primarily interested in the evaluation of acts – or should they focus instead on rules, character, motives or institutions? We will see that many of the differences between classical utilitarianism and contemporary utilitarianism can be explained by the shift from Bentham's focus on the evaluation of institutions to the modern focus on the evaluation of acts. We focus especially on contemporary *rule-utilitarianism* – the theory that, instead of calculating the consequences of each individual act, you should aim to follow the best utilitarian code of rules. We ask what that code might look like, and assess its intuitive plausibility.

Chapter 7 focuses on another feature of utilitarianism that is attracting considerable attention in current moral theory: the fact that utilitarianism assumes that the only rational response to value is to *promote* it – to produce as much as possible of whatever is valuable. Indeed, this *consequentialist* principle is often presented as the defining feature of the whole utilitarian tradition, with classical utilitarianism being just one form of consequentialism. Utilitarianism *is* consequentialism (morality promotes value) *plus* welfarism (value is aggregate human welfare). We ask whether utilitarians can improve the appeal of their theory by departing from consequentialism. We also explore alternative responses to value, particularly the notion of honouring or respecting value (made famous – among philosophers – by the eighteenth-century German philosopher Immanuel Kant), and a variety of alternative responses advocated by contemporary virtue ethicists, such as expressing value, embodying value, nurturing value and so on.

One enduring criticism of utilitarianism has always been that, as it rests upon precise calculations of utility, it is unworkable. Chapter 8 explores this objection, with a focus on the following questions. Can happiness be measured? Does utilitarianism presuppose that happiness can be measured? How does utilitarianism deal with uncertainty? What guidance does utilitarianism offer in the real world?

Finally, Chapter 9 explores two emerging debates in contemporary utilitarianism – the possibility of a genuinely global ethic, and the nature of our obligations to future generations. The underlying theme of the chapter is that utilitarianism has always been, and continues to be, most interesting and most relevant when applied to changing social circumstances, or to issues that have been under-appreciated by other moral theories.

two

Classical utilitarianism

The early utilitarians

Utilitarian ideas are found in many philosophers down the centuries – from the ancient Greeks through to the leading figures of the Scottish Enlightenment (especially David Hume and Adam Smith). However, utilitarianism only became clearly identified as a distinct philosophical school in the late eighteenth century. The three most prominent early utilitarians published their major works within a few years of one another: William Paley in 1785, Jeremy Bentham in 1789, and William Godwin in 1793. All three thinkers shared the values of the Enlightenment – a Europe-wide intellectual and cultural movement characterized by faith in human reason, opposition to arbitrary authority in law, government or religion, and belief in progress. Today Bentham is the most famous. At the time, however, he was much less well known than Paley and Godwin, who both reached a comparatively wide audience.

William Paley (1743–1805), a minister in the Church of England, offered utilitarianism as a way to determine the will of God. God, being benevolent, would want us all to act in the way that best promotes the general happiness. While he was radical on some issues, notably his fierce opposition to slavery, Paley's general tendency was conservative, especially regarding property. The best way to promote the general happiness was to follow the established laws of property.

In the nineteenth century, despite Paley's conservatism, utilitarianism was associated with political extremists and atheists. This was due to the influence of William Godwin (1756–1836) and Jeremy Bentham (1748–1832). Godwin was a social and political radical, who defended an extreme version of utilitarianism: a completely impartial morality, with no place for special obligations or attachments to our nearest and dearest. Godwin delighted in presenting his views in terms designed to shock his contemporaries. Here is one notorious example.

The Archbishop and the chambermaid
You are trapped in a burning building with two other people. One is an Archbishop who is "a great benefactor of mankind" and the other is a chambermaid. You only have time to save one person from the fire. What should you do?

Godwin concludes that you should save the Archbishop, as his life is of more value to human happiness than the chambermaid's. This remains true even if the chambermaid is your own mother – or yourself!

It is not a coincidence that theological utilitarians tend to be more conservative than secular utilitarians. If the universe has been designed by a utilitarian God, then we should obviously expect it to be already very well organized to promote happiness. By contrast, both Godwin and Bentham would have regarded the inefficiency of modern legal and social structures as evidence against the existence of a benevolent deity.

Jeremy Bentham (1748–1832)

Jeremy Bentham was born in London, and lived most of his life there. He was the son and grandson of lawyers and was expected to practise law himself. Instead he spent his life trying to improve the law. Bentham described himself as a "hermit" – whether living in remote cottages or in London. He wrote a great deal, publishing only an *Introduction* and a *Fragment* of his vast uncompleted work. Bentham's views were thought-out in the second half of the eighteenth century, prior to the industrial revolution. However, he was almost completely ignored until 1802, when some of his works were translated into French. Bentham did not gain real prominence until his work was publicized in the 1830s by J. S. Mill. When he died, Bentham left 70,000 sheets of foolscap manuscript behind him – including much theoretical work, but also highly detailed designs for states, prisons, banknotes and much else. Bentham visited Russia, Poland and Germany. Along the way he witnessed a wide variety of social organizations, including the slave ships of the Turkish empire. These experiences led him to reflect both on the variety of possible social arrangements and on the key role of incentives. Bentham helped to establish the University of London. In his will, he stipulated that his body should be preserved so that he could always be present at meetings of the university senate.

Bentham's philosophy is in the *empiricist* tradition. All knowledge must ultimately be traced to *impressions* made on our senses by physical objects. He applied this empiricist principle to human action and society. His main interest was in the law. In the eighteenth century, almost all law was the creation of judges rather than Parliament. Bentham objected both to the content of the law of his day, and to the way it was made. He came increasingly to see the two as related. At first Bentham thought the law was an accidental incoherent jumble. Over the course of his life, he came to regard it as deliberately designed to further the interests of a small elite.

Bentham saw himself as offering advice to a legislator. He often took this quite literally, even travelling to Russia with the aim of offering instruction to the Empress Catherine the Great. (This project might have been more successful if Bentham had actually tried to meet the Empress, rather than burying himself in a cottage on an isolated estate to write.) In the eighteenth century, when Bentham began his career, absolute monarchy was the most common system of government in Europe. So he pictures the legislator as an absolute monarch: a single person whose word is law. (Bentham's frustration with absolute monarchs – who would not listen to him – later led him to champion democratic reform.)

The utilitarian principle

Bentham offers his legislator both a goal and a mountain of advice for meeting that goal. The goal is the *utilitarian principle*, or the *greatest happiness principle*. The legislator's job is to use her knowledge of human nature to design laws that maximize the happiness of her people. (Bentham often uses the technical term "utility". This word can mean different things in English. Bentham's meaning is approximately equivalent to "instrumental for happiness". However, Bentham also has a specific theory of what happiness is.)

Utilitarianism is the basis of Bentham's entire philosophy. It provides not only the content of that philosophy, but also its motivation. The only justification for engaging in theoretical speculation is its practical value. For instance, unlike many other early modern European philosophers, Bentham was not at all troubled by scepticism about the external world, about other minds, or about morality. He takes it for granted that he exists, together with his body, his pen and the whole natural world, including other people. His justification is utilitarian:

> No bad consequences can possibly arise from supposing it to be true and the worst consequences cannot but arise from supposing it to be false.
> (Bentham Manuscripts at University College London, quoted in Harrison, *Bentham*, 54)

Along with utilitarianism, Bentham endorses *hedonism* – the view that pleasure and pain are the foundation of morality.

> By utility is meant the property in any object, whereby it tends to produce benefit, advantage, pleasure, or happiness, (all this in the present case comes to the same thing) or (what comes again to the same thing) to prevent the happening of mischief, pain, evil or unhappiness.
> (Bentham, "Introduction to the Principles of Morals and Legislation", [1789], quoted in Singer (ed.), *Ethics*, 307)

The value of a pleasure is entirely determined by seven measures of quantity: intensity, duration, certainty or uncertainty, propinquity or remoteness, fecundity, purity and extent. Bentham notoriously treats all pleasures as equally valuable.

> Prejudice apart, the game of pushpin is of equal value with the arts and sciences of music and poetry.
> (*ibid.*, quoted in Singer (ed.), *Ethics*, 200)

When he makes such comments, however, Bentham is not offering advice to individuals on how to live their lives. Rather, he is advising the legislator. His point is not that all pleasures really are equally valuable, but that the *legislator* has no business favouring some pleasures over others. In practice, with one or two notable exceptions, the legislator should regard people's preferences as the most reliable guide to their happiness. (Many contemporary liberal philosophers would agree with this claim, without necessarily thinking that all pleasures are actually equally valuable.)

It is unfortunate that Bentham uses poetry as his example. Bentham himself did not like poetry – he thought poets were dishonest because they knew that what they said was not true. But he was not the philistine you often see in caricatures of utilitarianism. Bentham was very fond of music, and was an accomplished keyboard player. Yet he would still say the sovereign should not favour good music over bad.

Some opponents of utilitarianism argue that the theory would approve of slavery, so long as the slaves were happy. Bentham strenuously denied this. The choices of human beings are our best information as to what makes people happy. As no one ever voluntarily chooses slavery, we should conclude that slaves are never happy.

Another notorious feature of Bentham's utilitarianism is its appeal to "the greatest happiness of the greatest number". In subsequent philosophical discussion, this principle has often been taken to mean that utilitarianism sacrifices the unfortunate few to the powerful many (Chapter 5). For instance utilitarianism might still favour slavery if the unhappiness of slaves is outweighed by the economic benefits slavery provides to other people. When Bentham uses the phrase "the greatest happiness of the greatest number", however, he invariably means either (a) the interests of the powerless many should take precedence over the interests of the powerful few, or (b) if a certain benefit cannot be provided to everyone, then it should be provided to as many people as possible.

Utilitarianism is often presented as a philosophy of calculation, assigning precise values to different pleasures (in units or "hedons") and calculating their exact probabilities. Bentham's writings often encourage this impression. He speaks of utilitarianism as a "scientific morality". However, Bentham was mainly interested in sciences involving classification (such as botany and geology) rather than calculation (such as mathematics and physics). His "scientific" morality involves detailed lists of types of pleasures, and of things that tend to produce pleasure – rather than exact calculations of quantities of pleasure.

Like everything else he wrote, Bentham's lists of pleasures were produced for a particular purpose. Legal rules must be applied to particular cases by individual judges. So Bentham offers the legislator a list of factors for judges to consider – factors correlated with pleasure and pain – rather than prescribing specific punishments for every possible offence. Bentham explicitly denies that judges (or anyone else) should apply the utilitarian principle on every separate occasion.

> It is not to be expected that this process should be strictly pursued previously to every moral judgement, or in every legislative or judicial operation. It must, however, be always kept in view.
>
> (Bentham, *ibid.*, quoted in Singer (ed.), *Ethics*, 312)

Modern hedonism faces many difficulties, as we will see in Chapter 4. Most of these would not bother Bentham. For his broad social purposes, it is sufficient to know that pleasure is good, that each person's pleasure is equally important, and that some ways of organizing society clearly tend to produce more pleasure than others.

Why choose the utilitarian principle?

There are many possible goals a legislator might adopt. Why should they choose the utilitarian principle? Bentham's main defence is offence. Utilitarianism provides a possible moral basis for legislation, and nothing else does. The dominant view in British moral philosophy in the eighteenth century was that we discover the moral truth by consulting our "moral sense" or "sentiments". Bentham objects that sentiments cannot provide a reliable universal foundation for morality. Each person's sentiments follow their own interests, rather than the interests of all. To base morality on sentiment is to base it on "caprice". Such a morality must either be "despotic" (if one person's feelings are imposed on everyone) or "chaotic" (if everyone uses their own feelings as a moral guide).

One obvious alternative is for the legislator to follow the will of God. Surely we should have the laws God would want us to have. Bentham himself was an atheist, at least in later years. However, as all legislators in his day were religious, he did not want to offer advice only to atheist legislators. So Bentham borrows an argument from theological utilitarians such as William Paley. Even if we seek to follow the word of God, we should be guided by the utilitarian principle. If God is good, then

God will want what is best for human beings. As God loves all human beings equally, God will want us to follow the utilitarian principle, rather than privileging the interests of any one small group. Bentham also argues that we know what gives people pleasure and pain far better than we know the will of God. Any legislator claiming to follow the will of God is really only following his own sentiments (or his own interests).

Another popular alternative at the time was to base law on *natural rights*. (This often went together with an appeal to God – natural rights were the rights God had given to human beings.) Bentham's attack on natural rights is one of his most influential themes. It begins with the notion of a *fiction*. The law of Bentham's day contained a very limited number of "causes of action" – grounds on which a case could be brought to court. Often, although it was obviously desirable for a case to be heard, no cause of action was available if the case was honestly described. So judges and lawyers deliberately misrepresented the facts – pretending the case was one that could be heard. This was known as a "legal fiction". Bentham thought these fictions were dishonest, and not a satisfactory substitute for an open and honest legal system based on the utilitarian principle. He wrote of William Blackstone (a contemporary defender of the Common Law tradition):

> To purge the science [of legislation] of the poison introduced into it by him, and those who write as he does, I know but of one remedy . . . by definition, perpetual and regular definition.
>
> (Bentham, *A Comment on the Commentaries*, 346, quoted in Harrison, *Bentham*, 52)

> [Instead of precedent and fiction] the science of legislation ought to be built on the immovable basis of sensations and experience.
>
> (Bentham Manuscripts at University College London, quoted in Harrison, *Bentham*, 141)

However, Bentham puts the notion of a legal fiction to his own use, by developing a *philosophical* notion of fiction, with much wider application. A fiction is any term that seems to refer to an entity that does not exist. ("Santa Claus" and "Bob's right not to be tortured" are, for

Bentham, both fictional terms.) Fictional terms are not all useless. Faced with a statement involving fictional terms, the philosopher aims to provide an analysis in terms of objects that do exist. Ultimately, we arrive at claims about particular sense experiences. If this succeeds, then we have a benign fictional term – one that has a clear and useful meaning. If not, then we conclude that the entity in question is not only fictional but *fabulous* – and thus we abandon the fiction. Bentham compares fictions to paper money, a new innovation at the time. If we know how to exchange the paper currency for real money (gold), then it is a genuine currency. If there is no gold to be had, then the paper is worthless.

For instance, *legal rights* are a benign fiction. We can explain my legal right to eat my chocolate bar in terms of the duty of others to allow me to eat it, the duty of the police to prevent anyone interfering with my eating and so on. These duties can, in their turn, be analysed into the punishments or sanctions people suffer if they do not fulfil their duties. The language of legal rights is thus reducible, ultimately, to the language of pleasure and pain.

Natural rights, on the other hand, are fabulous entities and talk of them is pure "nonsense". They claim to be written into the moral fabric of the universe, and to take precedence over the laws or customs of any particular country. Yet the very idea of a right can only be analysed in terms of a particular system of law that actually exists. The notion of natural rights that are pre-legal or supra-legal makes no sense. Bentham is especially opposed to "imprescriptible natural rights" – rights that cannot be over-ridden by the legislator. He calls such rights "nonsense upon stilts", and regards them as one of the principal barriers to political and legal reform.

If I say someone has a natural right to something, then all this can mean is that I think they *should* be given a *legal* right to it. This second claim is always justified either by appealing to the individual's own interest or sentiments, or to the common good. Despite appearances to the contrary, all moral principles are defended either by a mere appeal to sentiment or by the utilitarian principle.

> When a man attempts to combat the principle of utility, it is with reasons drawn, without his being aware of it, from that very principle itself.
>
> (Bentham, "Introduction to the Principles of Morals and Legislation", quoted in Singer (ed.), *Ethics*, 308)

How does the utilitarian principle guide the legislator?

> Nature has placed mankind under the governance of two
> sovereign masters, pain and pleasure.
>
> (*ibid.*, quoted in Singer (ed.), *Ethics*, 306)

Bentham's advice to the legislator is based on *psychological hedonism*: the claim that people are *motivated* by pleasure and pain. Bentham clearly endorses both psychological hedonism and *ethical hedonism* (the claim that morality is all about the promotion of pleasure and the reduction of pain). However, the relationship between them is not clear. Sometimes Bentham suggests that psychological hedonism supports ethical hedonism. Morality must be based on pleasure and pain because these are people's only motivations. At other times, psychological hedonism is presented as merely a very useful fact the utilitarian legislator must take into account. To explore these complex issues, we focus on two key areas of social regulation: economic liberalism and the criminal law.

Bentham largely follows Adam Smith's defence of the free market. (Indeed, Bentham extended Smith's position by defending "usury" – the charging of market-based interest rates – which was illegal at the time.) People are the best judges of their own interests. Things go best overall if people are free to decide for themselves what to produce, what contracts to enter, and what to buy. More generally, the legislator should not interfere with the free choices of individuals.

The value of market freedom is *instrumental*, not *intrinsic*. Freedom is valued only because it contributes to pleasure. Bentham's support of the market is limited by the utilitarian principle. He was influenced by the observation that most actual government intervention in his day served merely to protect the interests of small powerful minorities, rather than safeguarding the broader interests of the majority.

However, people are not *infallible* judges of their own interests. Bentham does not *identify* an individual's interests with their preferences or choices, as some later utilitarian economists have done (Chapter 4). People can misunderstand their own interests. If the legislator knows that people generally make a certain kind of mistake, then he can and should intervene to encourage people to act according to their *real* interests, rather than their mistaken perception of their interests.

Bentham believes that one particular mistake is especially significant. People fail to realize that pleasures or pains in the far distant future are just as important as immediate pleasures and pains. This is why they fail to make adequate provision for their old age. Because this is a general feature of human beings, the legislator is better placed to know people's long-term interests than they are. (As a solution, Bentham proposed a form of currency that would automatically attract interest. This would force people to save, and also teach them the value of saving. Whenever possible, the legislator should improve people's motivations.)

People's most important interest is *security*. Bentham uses this term more broadly than we might. Security includes adequate food and shelter, as well as security against hostility. The importance of security justifies redistribution, respect for property rights, and the criminal law.

Since the nineteenth century, Bentham has been pictured mainly as a supporter of the free market. However, he actually imagines a much broader positive role for the state than almost all his contemporaries. The government must ensure that no one goes destitute, and that everyone has access to adequate education and health care, to enable them to meet their own security needs. It is hard for us to realize how radical this was: even when Bentham died, the British government still provided no public funding for education, and the ministries of health and education that he envisaged were not established until the early years of the twentieth century. The "Benthamite state" is much closer to the modern welfare state than to the minimalist state of either eighteenth-century reality or contemporary libertarian fantasy.

So long as people are not destitute, they can usually meet their own security interests. However, they can only do this effectively if they are able to make long-term plans. People require security of property. This creates a strong presumption in favour of the existing property system – even if an alternative system would be more efficient when considered in the abstract. This is another instance of Bentham's pragmatic focus.

Crime and punishment

In his day, Bentham was perhaps best known as a prison reformer. His account of punishment is purely utilitarian. The role of punishment is deterrence. The value of punishment is not the actual punishment but the threat of it. Actual punishment involves undesirable cost – the expense and the pain of the criminal. The ideal would be to create a

threat of punishment without ever punishing anyone. Un\
the only reliable way to create a credible threat of punishme\
ally to punish people. Prisons should be open to the publi\
everyone could see punishment being delivered. (The death p\
especially effective – because people mistake their own intere\ ...u
overestimate the pain involved in death!)

Bentham is famous for his advocacy of the *panopticon*: a prison where cells are arranged on various levels in a circle around a central observation point, enabling the maximum number of criminals to be managed by the minimum number of guards. Bentham originally introduced this idea in a light-hearted manner, as a solution for a wide variety of surveillance situations. (For instance, he suggested a panopticon Turkish harem – where the maximum number of wives could be monitored by the minimum number of eunuchs.) But he then spent many years attempting to get British government support and funding for his panopticon. In the end, all these schemes failed, and Bentham lost most of his inheritance. He was eventually granted £23,000 (a small fortune) by a special Act of Parliament for the expense he had incurred. (This was ironic, as Bentham was a lifelong opponent of exactly this sort of *ad hoc* personalized use of sovereign power. But he kept the money anyway.)

The panopticon, and the general idea of public punishment, also illustrates a broader feature of Bentham's advice to the legislator. Publicity not only deters criminals, it also keeps officials honest. Without publicity, there is no way the legislator can ensure that the interests of officials coincide with the public interest. Psychological hedonism applies to officials, just as much as to potential criminals. The legislator must always attend to the incentive effects of institutional design. (Adam Smith offered a similar criticism of the practice of universities offering salaries to professors, as it made the interests of professors contrary to the interests of their students. If students paid their teachers, then their interests would coincide.)

Psychological hedonism is not a universal law. Bentham was only too aware that people are often altruistic. (Indeed, his original attempts to sell his theory to legislators assumed that they, at least, must have some concern for the interests of others.) Yet legislators should *assume* universal egoism. Even if people are not completely egoistic, they are largely so. Actions completely unrelated to the agent's interests are the exception rather than the rule. Furthermore, whatever the truth about people's motivations, the legislator should adopt the most pessimistic assumption. If we design our institutions on the assumption that people always act only on their own interests, then we will not be disappointed. The presence of publicity will not deter those with altruistic motives, whereas the absence of publicity gives too much licence to unscrupulous officials.

In addition to reforming the criminal law in its traditional areas, Bentham sought to extend it to cover, among other things, obligations to animals and obligations to provide assistance to people in need (the so-called Good Samaritan legislation, often incorporated in the criminal codes of continental Europe). He also argued for the decriminalization of "victimless crimes" such as unconventional sexual activity. The utilitarian principle is to govern the scope of the criminal law, as well as its content.

Who guards the guardians?

His lack of success in persuading monarchs and legislators to adopt his legal codes, and his frustrations over the panopticon proposal, led Bentham to question the motives of legislators. He came to believe that, just as prisons should be designed on the assumption that officials are primarily self-interested, we must make the same assumption about political leaders. The best political system would make the interests of rulers coincide with the interests of the people. This is more effective than relying on the benevolence of absolute monarchs. As people are generally the best judges of their own interests, and as each person is most concerned with her own interests, the best political system allows people to choose their own rulers on a periodic basis. Bentham compares the choice of a ruler to the purchasing of a shoe to show why utilitarianism requires democracy.

> It is not every man that can make a shoe; but when a shoe is made, every man can tell whether it fits him without much difficulty.
>
> (Bentham Manuscripts at University College London, quoted in Harrison, *Bentham*, 209)

Bentham thus became a strong advocate for extending the franchise to all adult males. This was radical at the time. The one exception Bentham explicitly defended was that the vote should not be given to those who could not read, as they would not have sufficient information to judge the performance of their rulers. (This was a much more significant exception then than now, as literacy rates were much lower than today.)

In private, Bentham admitted that there were no good reasons for not allowing women to vote. However, he refrained from defending this view in public, as he thought this would only lead to ridicule. We see again the supremacy of the utilitarian principle. When presenting one's view in public, one should be guided by *effectiveness* rather than truth.

A utilitarian reformer should direct his calls for democracy both to the existing elite and to the people as a whole. Without the support of the population, the existing system of government would not survive. Once the common people realize that democracy is in their interests, they will begin to demand it. Even if current leaders are completely self-interested, they will eventually share power rather than risk losing it altogether. (This claim was much more plausible in the nineteenth century than it might have been earlier, as all European monarchs were wary of the example of the French Revolution.)

Beyond legislation

While legislation was Bentham's main interest, he also wrote briefly about personal morality. His one work on this subject was only published posthumously, in a form that greatly disappointed his closest followers. The task of the "personal moralist" is to persuade people to do their duty by showing them that it coincides with their real interests. This is not because people are necessarily purely self-interested, nor because morality consists merely in enlightened self-interest. As ever, Bentham's motivations are pragmatic. The kind of persuasion he offers is the only kind of moralizing that can possibly hope to have any useful impact. His complaint against contemporary popular moralists, who mostly list pious principles, is not that what they say is untrue, but rather that, because it fails to engage people's self-interest, it has no impact.

Bentham's real legacy is not a set of (often idiosyncratic) proposals, but the general principle that law and public administration should be guided by the general interests of the public.

John Stuart Mill (1806–73)

Mill was born in London, and lived most of his life there. He was educated by his father, James Mill, himself an accomplished philosopher and a friend of Jeremy Bentham. The young Mill learnt the classics, logic, political economy, jurisprudence and psychology – starting with Greek at the age of three. Mill suffered a deep depression in his twenties. He recovered partly through reading poetry. Like his father, Mill worked for the East India Company – a private company in London which effectively ruled India. In 1851 Mill married Harriet Taylor, a long-time "friend" whose husband had recently died. Mill was a Member of Parliament for a short time in the 1860s. He was often involved in radical causes, especially women's rights. In addition to moral and political philosophy, Mill was best-known for his *System of Logic* (1843) and his *Principles of Political Economy* (1848).

Utilitarianism was Mill's religion. He was raised by his father in the utilitarian faith, and remained true to it all his life. Like many philosophers before and since, Mill sought to provide his religion with a philosophically sophisticated defence, informed by the main philosophical and cultural currents of his day.

Mill's general philosophy is a very strong form of *empiricism*. All knowledge is based on induction from experience. We know the sun will rise tomorrow only because we have seen it rise many times before. Mill denied the possibility of *a priori* knowledge – knowledge that is based entirely on reason and is thus prior to experience. (This feature of empiricism was a radical departure, as philosophy had traditionally been seen as the search for *a priori* knowledge.)

Mill's empiricism applied to all areas of knowledge, even mathematics and logic. "One plus one equals two" is a generalization from experience – it might conceivably be refuted by future experiences. In any area of knowledge, Mill has two aims: to explore all possible sources of empirical information and to refute the attempts of other philosophers to justify non-empirical knowledge. In *Utilitarianism*, Mill's empiricism is applied to several questions. Why should we be utilitarians? What is happiness? What makes human beings happy? How should society be organized?

Mill offers a new psychological and historical account of human beings. This leads to some very significant departures from the utilitarianism of Bentham. Many subsequent thinkers have argued that Mill effectively abandons utilitarianism. We might wonder whether Mill would have become a utilitarian if he had not been brought up as one.

Mill's "proof"

Mill was not satisfied with Bentham's indirect, and largely negative, defences of utilitarianism. He sought a *proof* of the utilitarian principle.

For an empiricist, this means deriving the principle from observation. This would give utilitarianism a sounder foundation than any of its opponents. Mill's chief opponents in ethics were *intuitionists* – for whom "the distinction between right and wrong is an ultimate and inexplicable fact, perceived by a special faculty known as a 'moral sense'" (Crisp, *Mill on Utilitarianism*, 8). Mill's proof is alarmingly brief:

> The only proof capable of being given that an object is visible, is that people actually see it. The only proof that a sound is audible, is that people hear it: and so of the other sources of our experience. In like manner . . . the sole evidence it is possible to produce that anything is desirable is that people do actually desire it . . . No reason can be given why the general happiness is desirable, except that each person . . . desires his own happiness. This, however, being a fact, we have not only all the proof which the case admits of, but all which it is possible to require, that happiness is a good: that each person's happiness is a good to that person, and the general happiness, therefore, a good to the aggregate of persons.
>
> (Mill, *Utilitarianism*, 81)

Mill's proof has three key steps.

1. The move from "people desire x" to "x is desirable".
2. The move from "the happiness of each person is good for him" to "the general happiness is a good for the aggregate of persons".
3. The claim that happiness is the *only* end: that everything we desire is either a *part* of happiness, or a *means* to happiness. (Without this step, we have not proved utilitarianism, but only the weak claim that happiness is one good thing – perhaps one among many.)

Generations of philosophers have cut their teeth exposing the fallacies of Mill's simple proof. In the early twentieth century, the Cambridge philosopher G. E. Moore accused Mill of committing the "naturalistic fallacy" – illegitimately attempting to derive an "ought" from an "is". While "visible" *means* "capable of being seen", "desirable" does *not* mean "*capable* of being desired". It means "*ought* to be desired". People might desire all sorts of things that are not desirable.

Moore is unfair to Mill, because he does not share Mill's notion of "proof". Moore expects a proof to be a watertight logical deduction. If we have proved something, then there must be no reasonable doubt whether it is true. As an empiricist, Mill is not so ambitious. He only seeks the best proof that experience can provide in a particular context. The fact that people desire chocolate does not make it logically impossible that chocolate is not desirable. But it does provide the only possible evidence, and thus the only possible "proof", that chocolate is desirable. Mill's main claim is negative: there are no other proofs. (Like Bentham, Mill is untroubled by scepticism. He assumes that the best proof must be good enough.)

If we want to refute Mill's proof in his own terms, we need an alternative route to knowledge of what is desirable. Moore himself offered a rather naive version of the moral sense approach. Mill follows Bentham in rejecting the very idea of a moral sense on empiricist grounds – we have no direct access to the property of desirability.

The second step of Mill's proof has become extremely controversial in recent utilitarian discussion. Mill is accused of ignoring the "separateness of persons", by treating "the aggregate of persons" as if it were a person. (We calculate the happiness of the aggregate by adding together the happiness of different people, just as we might calculate a person's total happiness by adding together the happiness she feels at different moments in her life.) Mill himself did not worry much about aggregation. All he seems to want to say is that, given that each person's happiness is a good for that person, the happiness of people in general is a good for society as a whole. This is enough to justify using the general happiness to evaluate moral rules.

The final step of Mill's proof is even more controversial. It is also the stage of the proof to which Mill himself devoted most of his attention. Most people would agree that happiness is a good thing. Yet is it the *only* good thing? To answer this question, we must ask what Mill means by "happiness". (We return to the other details of Mill's proof, and its place in the development of utilitarianism, in Chapter 3.)

What is happiness?

Utilitarianism is often attacked as crass and philistine – a complaint prompted by Bentham's infamous remark about the comparative merits of pushpin and poetry. The nineteenth-century British conservative Thomas Carlyle called it "a pig philosophy". Pigs could feel pleasure just as well as human beings. So, if pleasure is all that matters, then people might as well live like contented pigs. Such a philosophy is an insult to human dignity.

Like Bentham, Mill is a hedonist. Happiness is all that matters, and happiness simply *is* pleasure and the absence of pain. He states this very clearly.

> By happiness is intended pleasure, and the absence of pain; by unhappiness pain, and the privation of pleasure.
>
> (Mill, *Utilitarianism*, 55)

To counter Carlyle's objection, Mill offers a new account of pleasure. He begins by asking why it is objectionable to put a human life and a pig life on a par. The reason is that human beings are capable of much more valuable experiences than pigs. But this claim is perfectly consistent with hedonism.

> It is quite compatible with the principle of utility to recognise the fact, that some kinds of pleasure are more desirable and more valuable than others. It would be absurd that while, in establishing all other things, quality is considered as well as quantity, the establishment of pleasure should be supposed to depend on quantity alone.
>
> (Mill, *Utilitarianism*, 56)

Mill then introduces a distinction between *higher pleasures* and *lower pleasures*. This is perhaps the most controversial aspect of Mill's ethical philosophy. We will explore Mill's distinction using a simple tale.

The choice
You have two options for your evening: reading Homer's *Iliad* and watching Brad Pitt in *Troy*. Both will give you pleasure, but the two pleasures differ in several ways. Which should you choose?

For Bentham, the answer is simple. Whichever pleasure is more intense is the better one. Mill denies this. There is more to pleasure than its intensity. The adrenaline rush of enjoying a good action movie may be more intense than the feeling of reading poetry or philosophy, but the latter is the *higher* pleasure. To discover which pleasure is better, we must find a *competent judge*: someone who has experienced both.

People who have experienced both higher and lower pleasures prefer the higher. So higher pleasures are better.

> It is better to be a human being dissatisfied than a pig satisfied; better to be Socrates dissatisfied than a fool satisfied. And if the fool, or the pig, has a different opinion, it is because they only know their own side of the question. The other party to the comparison knows both sides.
>
> (Mill, *Utilitarianism*, 57)

The idea of the competent judge raises several puzzles. Does *anyone* who has experienced both kinds of pleasure count as a competent judge? If they do, then we cannot expect all competent judges to agree. People who were forced to read poetry (or philosophy) at school might honestly say that they much prefer watching Brad Pitt fight in a skirt. Mill could reply that such people have not really experienced the *pleasure* of poetry or philosophy, as they do not truly appreciate the experience. But this threatens to make our test circular. (How do we know that someone has "truly appreciated" philosophy? Because they prefer it to action movies.) Also, aficionados of action movies can reply that the problem with philosophers and poetry lovers is that *they* have not learnt to appreciate a good sword fight.

Perhaps Mill's best defence lies in his empiricism. The preferences of competent judges are not an infallible proof of the superiority of higher pleasures. But they are the only evidence we can possibly have. Unanimity is not essential – if most competent judges agree, then we still have some evidence. And there is simply no better evidence to be had.

> From this verdict of the only competent judges, I apprehend there can be no appeal.
>
> (Mill, *Utilitarianism*, 58)

As an empiricist, Mill is open to new information. If it turned out that competent judges tended to prefer action movies to philosophy, then he would have to accept that movies provide a higher pleasure. This does not undermine the claim that there are higher pleasures – it just redraws the boundary.

The puzzling thing about Mill's distinction is that he does not see it as a rejection of hedonism. Despite their lower degree of *intensity*, higher pleasures are *more pleasurable* than lower ones. The competent judge prefers reading philosophy because it is more pleasant, not for some other reason.

Mill's opponents have always argued that, once we admit the competent judge test, we ought to conclude that pleasure is not the only good. Competent judges often value other things more than pleasure – such as knowledge, status, or achievement. I might choose to read Mill's *Utilitarianism* rather than going to the new Brad Pitt movie, even though I know the movie would be more pleasant, because I value knowledge over pleasure. We return to these issues on pages 67–71 in Chapter 4.

Utilitarianism and customary morality

By the mid-nineteenth century, utilitarianism was associated in the public mind with dangerous political radicals and atheists. While Mill did defend some quite radical social and political ideas in the name of utilitarianism, he also wanted to show that the theory was often less radical than its opponents feared. Mill sought to bring utilitarianism closer to customary morality.

This may seem an impossible task. Surely utilitarianism tells us to make decisions, and to evaluate legislation and public policy, solely on the basis of an impersonal calculation of consequences. Wouldn't it be an astonishing coincidence if those calculations agreed with customary morality?

The theological utilitarians, such as Paley, had an easy reply. Customary morality is given us by God. God is a utilitarian. So whatever God gives us will be identical to the recommendations of utilitarianism. Mill's utilitarianism has no place for God. Like Bentham, Mill himself was probably an atheist. However, he did recognize that religion could play a positive role in society, by providing a sense of shared community and purpose. Nor did Mill defend atheism in public – perhaps for good utilitarian reasons. On the other hand, he certainly did not want his moral theory to rest on controversial religious claims. Instead of God, Mill appeals to history – in particular the fashionable nineteenth-century view that saw human history as evidence of evolution and progress. Customary morality has evolved to meet the needs of human societies. It thus reflects the judgements and experiments of countless generations, each seeking to promote the general happiness.

Our original problem was that utilitarianism was too radical. Mill now seems to have the opposite problem. If I depart from customary morality, I put my own judgement above the whole past judgement of mankind. But surely this level of self-assurance could never be justified. So I should never depart from customary morality. Utilitarianism is redundant.

Mill's solution is to locate the utilitarian principle *within* customary morality. The general rules of popular morality often come into conflict. For instance, customary morality tells me to always protect the innocent, and never tell lies. But what if a lie is the only way to save an innocent person's life? One of Mill's chief criticisms of his intuitionist opponents was that they provide no principled way to resolve such dilemmas. The utilitarian principle emerges as the best way to systematize the chaos of customary morality.

While Mill is more theoretically inclined than Bentham, his main interest is still in practical issues. Utilitarianism is not just a theory to be studied – it is a guide to life, especially public and political life. We now turn to four illustrations of Mill's application of the utilitarian principle. The first is from *Utilitarianism* itself, the other three from other works.

Justice

One of the most common objections to utilitarianism is that it cannot respect the rights of individuals. The utilitarian calculus may tell us to throw the Christians to the lions, or to punish an innocent person to prevent a riot by an angry mob. Mill replies that utilitarianism can accommodate our sense of justice. It can recognize rights.

Human beings have certain basic needs: for the essentials of life, for security, for shelter, for enough social stability to make future plans and so on. Mill follows Bentham in referring to these as "security" interests. These preconditions of a worthwhile life must be guaranteed to everyone as of right. I cannot enjoy security if I am worried that I may be deprived of the necessities of life by the government, or by some third party. So no one can enjoy security unless they live in a society where each individual has a *right to security*: a guarantee that their security interest will be met. There can be no good reason for meeting the security interests of some but not all. (At this point, Mill borrows a dictum from Bentham: "each is to count for one, and no one for more than one".) If the government follows the utilitarian principle in all individual cases, then no one enjoys a right to security and everyone is worse off.

The utilitarian principle tells us, not only how to act, but also how to think and feel. To ensure everyone's security, we must all feel bound to respect the rights of others, and not to apply the utilitarian principle when someone's security interests are at stake. Some recent philosophers have argued that, if utilitarianism tells us not to follow the utility principle, then the theory is either useless or incoherent. We return to this question in Chapter 6.

Does this utilitarian argument satisfy our sense of justice? The crucial test case is when a violation of one person's rights would save the lives of many others. Should we torture the terrorist's (innocent) child if this is the only way to get the terrorist to reveal the location of a bomb that threatens the lives of several million people? Utilitarians argue that, if we really know we are in this situation, then we ought to torture – if we can bring ourselves to do so. Opponents of utilitarianism disagree. We return to this question in Chapter 5.

Liberty

Mill's short essay *On Liberty* is one of the classic texts of political philosophy. In it, Mill defends the famous *liberty principle* (also known as the *harm principle*).

> The only purpose for which power can rightfully be exercised over any member of a civilised community, against his will, is to prevent harm to others. His own good, either physical or moral, is not a sufficient warrant.
>
> (Mill, *On Liberty*, 68)

Mill's basic strategy is to begin with one particular freedom that all his contemporaries would support, and then present the liberty principle as an extension, or perhaps only a clarification, of customary morality. Mill's example is religious freedom. In nineteenth-century England, the Church of England enjoyed very significant privileges. Many offices and professions were open only to its members, as were the universities. However, the general principle that people should be free to choose their own religion was almost universally accepted, and many respectable citizens were "non-conformists". No one wanted to return to the practice of earlier centuries, when the state tried to force people to join the established Church. In *On Liberty*, Mill tries to show how the arguments that justify religious freedom also justify a much broader liberty of lifestyle choice.

Mill wants his liberty principle to appeal to non-utilitarians as well as utilitarians. So he defends it, not on explicitly utilitarian grounds, but as an extension of principles drawn from customary morality. This raises an intriguing question. Is the liberty principle compatible with the utilitarian principle? The relationship between Mill's two principles has generated a huge literature. Some argue that the two principles are independent – Mill operates with two fundamental moral standards. On this view, *On Liberty* marks Mill's rejection of the utilitarianism of his father and Bentham. Others argue that the liberty principle is derived from the utility principle, and that Mill's reasons for not making this more explicit are themselves utilitarian. (He does not want people to reject his liberty principle because they are suspicious of its utilitarian origins.) Our focus is on Mill's utilitarianism. So we will explore possible utilitarian arguments he might offer for the liberty principle. The most interesting of these arguments relies on another aspect of Mill's complex account of happiness: the role of *individuality*. (As we shall see shortly, Mill also offers more conventional utilitarian arguments defending liberty on instrumental grounds. Even if freedom is not good in itself, it is the best way to promote other goods. For Mill, this means other pleasures.)

Mill believed that all knowledge arose from the "association" of ideas presented to the senses. (This *associationist* psychology was another inheritance from his father.) Everyone is equally capable of acquiring knowledge – no one is born with an innately superior intellect. Mill's own upbringing taught him that people are capable of much more development than is normally thought. The way to maximize happiness is thus not to give people what they now want, but to encourage them to have better wants. If higher pleasures are better than lower, we should aim for a world where everyone enjoys the higher pleasures – even if their ignorance prevents them from wanting higher pleasures at present.

Utilitarianism now threatens to be extremely paternalistic – forcing people to do things they do not want. Yet Mill himself is extremely anti-paternalistic, as the liberty principle shows. This is partly due to his notion of individuality. Mill's overriding lifelong ambition was to bring together the works of two thinkers he regarded as "the two great seminal minds of England of their age." (Schneewind, *Sidgwick and Victorian Moral Philosophy*, 130 – quoting Mill's own assessment of Bentham, originally published in 1838). One of these was Jeremy Bentham, the other was the poet and philosopher Samuel Taylor Coleridge (1772–1834). Coleridge was an opponent of utilitarianism, and of the Enlightenment in general. He was one of the intellectual leaders of the Romantic movement, and did more than anyone else to bring German philosophy to England – especially the works of Kant, Hegel and other German Romantics and Idealists.

Mill learnt two key lessons from Coleridge and the German Romantics: the historical evolution of culture, and the importance of individuality to human well-being. Mill does not mean by "individuality" exactly what we might mean today. "Autonomy" and "authenticity" are more accurate terms for us, though Mill does not use either term himself. The core idea is of living your own life according to values you identify with, as opposed to either having your life chosen for you or choosing unthinkingly. A human life is only truly valuable if it is lived in the right way.

Individuality seems very non-hedonistic. What counts is not the pleasures a life contains, but the way it is lived. In more recent moral philosophy, an emphasis on autonomy or authenticity is often seen as the antithesis of utilitarianism. Mill, however, wants to incorporate individuality into his hedonism. Individuality makes experiences more pleasant. (Mill again appeals to the competent judge. No one who has experienced an autonomous or authentic life would prefer an inauthentic life. No one who has been free would want to be a slave. No one who has seen the real world can be satisfied with life in the Matrix.)

There are several ways individuality might improve pleasure. It might be an extra *component* of value, or a *precondition* of value. If individuality is merely a component, then a life without individuality can still be very worthwhile. If individuality is a precondition, then a life without individuality cannot be worthwhile, no matter what else it contains. On this view, the value of the higher pleasures *depends* on their being autonomously pursued. This would explain why the person who is forced to read philosophy does not experience the pleasure of philosophy. It would also explain why human life is more valuable than pig life. Because they cannot be autonomous, pigs cannot be given the higher pleasures. However, Mill himself does not seem to endorse the stronger, precondition claim about individuality. As the title of Chapter 3 of *On Liberty* suggests, individuality is only one element of well-being, albeit a very important one. We return to these issues in Chapter 4.

Due to individual differences, people will exercise their individuality in different ways. Individuality thus results in diversity. It also *requires* diversity. The most important way we express our individuality is by choosing a style of living. Because we are social beings, a style of living requires a social context. We need a variety of lifestyles to choose from. Each person's "experiment in living" is not only an expression of their own individuality. It also provides a necessary background for the individuality of others. In a world of conformity, there could be no meaningful choice *for anyone*. The connection between individual well-being and social context is a central theme for Mill, and the key to understanding the connection between his moral philosophy and his political philosophy.

The liberty principle only covers self-regarding acts – those that do not affect anyone else. It does not say that we have complete freedom when our actions *do* affect others. But nor does it say that we are *only* free in the self-regarding sphere. Beyond that sphere, the liberty principle is simply silent. Once we leave the special sphere of the liberty principle, Mill's arguments for freedom become more clearly utilitarian. We examine two: freedom of expression and the freedom of market.

Mill's two utilitarian arguments for freedom of expression nicely illustrate both his empiricism and his interest in the historical context of ideas.

1. *Do not silence the truth.* We should not silence a view we disagree with, because we cannot be sure that it does not contain at least part of the truth. If I *silence* a view (rather than merely disagreeing with it), then I must be assuming that I am *infallible*. Empiricists deny that anyone is infallible.
2. *Do not silence falsehood.* Even if we were sure that a dissenting view was false, we still should not silence it. Dissenting views keep the orthodox view *alive*. If dissent is silenced, then people cannot test their belief by considering objections and alternatives. In the long run, belief becomes dead dogma. To illustrate this, Mill unfavourably compares the faith of nineteenth-century English Christians with that of the early Christians, who were constantly confronted with the arguments of non-Christian thinkers.

In his lifetime, Mill was best known as an expert on *political economy* – what we now call economics. He wrote a hugely influential textbook on the subject. In broad detail, his position is similar to Bentham's. Mill offers explicitly utilitarian arguments for the free market. Everyone is better off in the long run if people are left to make consumption and production decisions for themselves, and if goods and services are allocated by the market rather than by state control.

However, market freedom has definite limits. Mill explicitly acknowledges that market transactions are not self-regarding, because they have an impact on others. They are thus governed by the utility principle, and not the liberty principle. So government intervention is not ruled out – and Mill defends health and safety regulations, rules to prevent unfair monopolies, and other cases of interference in the market. In his later years, Mill became increasingly sympathetic to socialism, as he became disillusioned with the inequalities produced by unfettered capitalism and with the impact of industrialization on people's individuality.

Democracy

Mill was more wary of democracy than Bentham, perhaps because he had more experience of how it actually works. Earlier thinkers, who lived under absolute monarchs, had identified liberty with participation in the government. The threat to liberty was despotism, and democracy was the solution. One of Mill's main aims in *On Liberty* is to point out that, even in a democracy, liberty could be under threat from the forces of social conformity ("the tyranny of the majority"). Democracy does not guarantee liberty.

However, Mill did strongly favour democracy over alternative systems of government. In his long essay *Considerations on Representative Government*, he defends broader political participation on both instrumental and intrinsic grounds. Mill's instrumental argument is similar to Bentham's, and also to the standard utilitarian defence of the free market. People are the best judges of their own interests. Representative democracy is the best way to keep rulers honest, and to keep them focused on the interests of the majority.

Even if a benevolent dictator could do a perfect job of meeting people's interests, Mill would *still* prefer democracy. Political participation is good in itself – it promotes the self-development of citizens, especially those in menial occupations. The opportunity to participate in political decisions would give such people the incentive to concern themselves with the wider world, focus their minds on larger issues, and develop their capacity for making important decisions.

Mill favours *representative democracy* (where people elect representatives who then govern in their name) over *direct democracy* (where everyone votes on each particular decision). The representative version is more efficient. It permits some to specialize in the complex business of government, and leaves others free to devote their time to the more important things in life. (A distinguishing feature of Mill's political philosophy, in contrast to many earlier thinkers, is that he does not regard politics as the most important area of life.) As Bentham might have said, defenders of direct democracy are like people who want everyone to make their own shoes.

One feature of Mill's view seems quaint today. He defends a differential voting system, where those with more education would get more votes. (Unfortunately, Mill never explains how this would work. For instance, how would he deal with those – like himself – who are very well educated but lack any formal qualifications?)

The status of women

The most radical views Mill expressed in public concern the status of women. He argues that women should be given the vote, and otherwise treated as the political equals of men. Mill defends the rights of women by extending the principles of customary morality. In any other area of life, it would be considered completely unacceptable for people to be (a) forced into permanent contracts by a complete lack of alternatives, and then (b) not allowed to break or end those contracts. Mill then asks: why should the situation of married women be treated differently? (Mill's personal situation made him especially conscious of the desirability of allowing women to get divorced more easily!)

Mill's discussion of women also highlights his empiricism. His opponents claimed that women's social roles are suited to their nature. Mill replies that, precisely *because* of their limited social opportunities, we do not know much about women's nature. We simply cannot say whether women could benefit from higher education, or succeed in certain professions. So there is no good reason for not letting them try.

Mill was the last utilitarian, and perhaps the last English-speaking philosopher, who was also a major cultural figure. In philosophy itself, Mill fell out of favour in the early twentieth century, when his optimism and empiricism were both thought naive and out of date. However, in recent years Mill's writings across a wide range of areas – from logic and theory of knowledge to politics and economics – have been re-evaluated by contemporary theorists. In particular, for our purposes, we shall see that contemporary philosophy owes much to Mill, especially in moral and political philosophy.

Henry Sidgwick (1838–1900)

Sidgwick was born and died during the reign of Queen Victoria, and spent his entire adult life at Cambridge University, where he become

Knightbridge Professor of Moral Philosophy in 1883. He began as a classicist, but his intellectual interests were very broad, covering moral theory, metaphysics, politics and economics. Sidgwick was also deeply interested in religious questions, devoting much of his time to historical biblical criticism and psychic research. Indeed, he was a founder and the first president of the Society for Psychical Research. Although very well connected (one brother-in-law became Prime Minister and another was Archbishop of Canterbury), Sidgwick was never as active in politics as either Bentham or Mill. However, he did have considerable impact on academic affairs in Cambridge. Sidgwick was influential in the establishment of Newnham College, one of the first Oxbridge colleges open to women. In 1869, Sidgwick resigned his fellowship at Trinity College because he could no longer subscribe to the Thirty-Nine Articles of the Church of England – as all fellows were required to do. This requirement was abolished in 1871, partly due to Sidgwick's example.

Bentham, Mill and Sidgwick: differences and similarities

Sidgwick was the last of the great classical utilitarians. He is also, in many ways, the first modern moral philosopher. Sidgwick is much closer than either Bentham or Mill to the concerns and mindset of contemporary philosophers. Unlike both Bentham and Mill, Sidgwick was a professional academic philosopher – teaching in a university and writing primarily for academic publications. His philosophical writing focuses on the theory of ethics, and on the history of moral philosophy. While Sidgwick was quite active in public life, especially in the campaign to expand educational opportunities for women, he remained largely silent about the practical implications of his own philosophy. As we shall see, this silence itself follows from his philosophical conclusions.

Unlike his utilitarian predecessors, Sidgwick takes the threat of moral scepticism very seriously. One of his main worries is whether morality can survive the decline of religion. This is partly a practical concern: could a secular worldview replace religion as the social glue that holds society together? It also had a theoretical aspect: does morality even make sense in the absence of religion? Sidgwick is much less optimistic here than either Bentham or Mill. He believes that the decline of religion undermines non-utilitarian moral theory, and leads to a crisis for utilitarianism.

Like Mill, Sidgwick was influenced by current thought in Germany. In his case, the influence was much more philosophical. All that Mill borrowed from the German Romantics was a richer account of human nature, and especially its emotional, historical and social aspects. He retained a very British commitment to empiricism and induction. By contrast, Sidgwick's whole philosophical outlook was influenced by German philosophers, especially Immanuel Kant (1724–1804). While he remains sympathetic to the empiricist tradition, Sidgwick gives much more prominence to the idea of *reason*. His project is to base ethics on reason, rather than merely on empirical observation.

Like both Bentham and Mill, Sidgwick identifies himself as a hedonist. The only thing that is ultimately valuable is "desirable consciousness". To take an example later used against Sidgwick by his student G. E. Moore, consider two possible universes with no sentient creatures: one universe is very beautiful, the other very ugly. According to Sidgwick, as there is no observer to gain pleasure or pain, neither of these universes has any value whatsoever. The beautiful universe is no better than the ugly one.

Finally, Sidgwick had an elitist view of the social world, which sometimes shows through in his utilitarianism. The elite should use the utilitarian principle to design public institutions and moral rules, but the masses should be taught to obey those institutions and rules, and not to apply the utilitarian principle for themselves. (Bernard Williams, an influential late twentieth-century critic of utilitarianism, dubs this elitism "Government House Utilitarianism", on the grounds that it stems from the same arrogant attitude as the paternalistic government of British colonies in the nineteenth century.)

Utilitarianism and intuitionism

Sidgwick follows Mill in emphasizing the compatibility of utilitarianism and common-sense morality. Sidgwick called his masterpiece *The Methods of Ethics*. A method is a very general way of deciding what to do. Methods give rise to *principles* – more specific guides to action, such as the everyday rules of morality. Sidgwick isolates three possible methods of ethics: utilitarianism, intuitionism and egoism. In Sidgwick's time, as in Mill's, the main opponents of utilitarianism were intuitionists who believed in a "moral sense" giving us infallible knowledge of moral principles. (Sidgwick distinguishes *dogmatic* intuitionism – which he condemns – from *philosophical* intuitionism – which is the name he gives to his own methodology.)

Sidgwick's first task is to demonstrate the superiority of utilitarianism to intuitionism. The bulk of his book is a very detailed account of the basic principles of common-sense morality: wisdom, benevolence, justice, promise-keeping, truth-telling, self-regarding virtues, courage, humility and other virtues. Sidgwick's analyses have been a great inspiration to later generations of utilitarians. In each case, Sidgwick argues that intuitionism cannot deliver precise principles to guide our actions. Sidgwick agrees that a moral sense would give us moral certainty. If I had a moral sense, I would always know what to do. However, he uses this very fact to argue against the idea of a moral sense. As I often do not know what I ought to do, I obviously do *not* have a moral sense. As this is true of everyone, no one has a moral sense. So the intuitionist method falls apart. Only utilitarianism can deliver precise action-guiding principles. Because it traces them back to the utilitarian principle, utilitarianism also tells us *why* particular principles are correct.

Sidgwick's approach raises three broad questions.

1. *Does utilitarianism really capture the whole of customary morality?* For instance, as with Mill's theory, we might ask whether a utilitarian really can account for our sense of justice. Sidgwick himself argues that the main dispute between utilitarians and their opponents concerns benevolence. Everyone agrees that we have some obligation to assist others, but there is no consensus over the scope of that obligation. As we shall see in Chapter 5, opponents of utilitarianism still object to its account of benevolence.

2. *Are Sidgwick's three options exhaustive?* Opponents of utilitarianism have often argued that, because he starts with a broadly utilitarian worldview, Sidgwick misses a number of other possible methods, by lumping all alternatives to utilitarianism (apart from egoism) together as "(dogmatic) intuitionism", and then offering a quite narrow account of intuitionist morality.

   Sidgwick claims that every method must have an *end*: an ultimate source of value. For utilitarianism and egoism, this is pleasure – either pleasure in general, or my own pleasure. The alternative possible end is "human perfection". The moral theory with this end is intuitionism – because its moral rules are derived from an ideal of behaviour that would perfect human nature. (Sidgwick has in mind intuitionists whose perfectionism goes along with the view that morality consists in following God's pattern for our lives.)

   By identifying non-utilitarianism with intuitionism, and then tying intuitionism to perfectionism, Sidgwick thus ignores three possibilities: non-intuitionist perfectionism, non-perfectionist intuitionism, and alternatives to both utilitarianism and intuitionism. (An example of the first of these is *consequentialist perfectionism*: a theory like utilitarianism except that perfection replaces pleasure. Instead of maximizing pleasure, we maximize perfection. This option has been pursued in recent years by the Canadian philosopher Thomas Hurka.)

Much of twentieth-century moral philosophy is the search for additional non-utilitarian methods. The most prominent example is Rawls' rediscovery of Kant's *moral constructivism*. Rawls himself explicitly presents his theory as an alternative to both utilitarianism and intuitionism, in Sidgwick's sense. Rawls asks us to imagine what principles we would choose if we did not know who we would be. This "original position" forces us to focus on our obligations to one another as rational beings, abstracting from our particular concerns and interests. The aim is to provide a non-utilitarian foundation for moral principles. Other non-utilitarians defend modern versions of intuitionism, minus the perfectionism to which Sidgwick objected.

In theory, Sidgwick would not have been too troubled by these developments. His investigation is deliberately tentative and preliminary. If other people came up with new methods, or with new versions of old methods, then he would have welcomed the challenge of comparing these to utilitarianism and egoism.

3. *Must ethics have a method?* Many recent moral philosophers, especially Bernard Williams and various virtue ethicists, question the impulse to produce a complete moral system. This possibility is particularly important once we see that Sidgwick's own attempt to systematize ethics ended in chaos.

The dualism of practical reason

Once he has disposed of intuitionism, Sidgwick is left with two competing forms of hedonism: universalistic hedonism (utilitarianism) and egoistic hedonism (egoism). These tell me to maximize the general happiness and to maximize my own happiness. Sidgwick concludes that each method is an independently rational first principle. Neither takes precedence over the other. Unless the universe is "friendly" – unless it is specifically designed to make the two methods coincide – it seems clear that they will often conflict in practice. Suppose I have £10. I can maximize *my own* happiness by buying a movie ticket to see

Gratuitous Violence IV, but if I were maximizing *the general happiness* I could certainly find a better use for the money. At this point, reason offers no further guidance. Sidgwick finds an irresolvable *dualism* at the heart of human reason.

Sidgwick's dualism is related to the common objection that utilitarianism is extremely demanding (Chapter 5). However, Sidgwick has a deeper point. He finds a *contradiction* in practical reason, not just a moral difficulty. He is not just pointing out that our personal interests conflict with the general good, or that utilitarianism may be very demanding, or even that it may be psychologically impossible to comply with the demands of utilitarianism. Instead, he is saying that putting my own interests first is not just psychologically natural – it is also completely rational and unobjectionable. A completely selfish person cannot be convicted of any rational error.

For Sidgwick, the dualism of practical reason signals the failure of ethical theory. If moral philosophy is to succeed, it must reconcile the two methods. It is worth pausing to note how strong this requirement is. The contradiction in rationality is only avoided if every person's happiness always coincides exactly with the general happiness. Most of the rest of this book deals with cases where people's interests are in conflict – and so does most of everyday life. Without conflict, what would be left of ethics? A solution to Sidgwick's dualism would dissolve the main objections to utilitarianism, and perhaps remove all moral problems altogether. Sidgwick rejects all philosophical solutions to his dualism: religious, empiricist, Hegelian, Kantian and sceptical. This leads him to explore a paranormal alternative.

1. *The God solution.* The traditional solution was God. If God governs the universe, then we can be confident that we will be rewarded for doing our duty. So happiness and morality must coincide. Sidgwick agrees that this solution would be satisfactory. Unfortunately, we cannot be sure that God exists. (Our uncertainty about God is a further reason for rejecting intuitionism, which traditionally assumes that God has given us an infallible moral sense.) Sidgwick thus has much in common with earlier religious thinkers who argue that God is necessary to make sense of morality. We now see why Sidgwick is less optimistic than Mill that morality can survive the loss of religious faith. We also see why Sidgwick kept his own religious doubts to himself. If religious faith is necessary to avoid the dualism of practical reason, then widespread religious doubt is potentially disastrous.

2. *The empiricist solution.* Mill, following many contemporary sociologists, argued that, as society progresses, the interests of different people will come to coincide more and more. Mill's concern is practical. He seeks a society where people will act for the common good, even if they are naturally egoistic. Mill can thus afford some divergences between individual and general happiness, so long as the two typically coincide. Sidgwick's purpose is different from Mill's. Only a perfect coincidence will do. It is thus not surprising that Sidgwick draws a negative conclusion from his own empirical inquiries – the interests of individuals diverge too much from the general good.

3. *The Hegelian solution.* The British Hegelians – associated especially with Sidgwick's school friend T. H. Green (1836–82) at Oxford – based ethics on the metaphysics of G. W. F. Hegel (1770–1831), a very influential early nineteenth-century German philosopher. Hegel's metaphysics is notoriously hard to understand, but one key claim is that all dichotomies and distinctions are ultimately unreal. If we saw the universe correctly, we would recognize that the distinction between human individuals is an illusion – there are no separate individuals, merely aspects of a single eternal Absolute. The very idea of a divergence of interests is thus metaphysically incoherent. This basic *idealist* picture was very influential in British philosophy in the late nineteenth century. It fell out of favour at the start of the twentieth century – largely due to devastating attacks from two students of Sidgwick: Bertrand Russell (1872–1970) and G. E. Moore (1873–1958).

Although sympathetic to German philosophy, Sidgwick was still enough of an empiricist to believe that only an extremely strong argument could outweigh the compelling empirical evidence of a conflict between individual and general happiness. The arguments supporting Hegelian metaphysics were just not strong enough. (Indeed, despite his respect for his friend Green, Sidgwick found Hegelian metaphysics largely unintelligible.)

4. *The Kantian solution.* The Kantian solution is based on Kant's "moral argument" for belief in God and immortality. Theoretical speculation is based on our concepts, which are designed solely for the world we experience. Such speculation cannot take us beyond the world of experience. So it cannot tell us whether God exists, or whether we are immortal. However, morality tells me to aim for my own moral perfection and for a just world.

These demands are incoherent and irrational unless there is an afterlife presided over by a benevolent deity. Belief in God is morally necessary. We have practical reasons to believe in God, and no theoretical reason not to. Therefore, belief in God is reasonable.

Sidgwick was sometimes attracted to Kant's argument. In the end, however, he rejected it emphatically. Our need to systematize ethics gives us an urgent reason to *hope* that the universe is user-friendly, and provides a very strong motivation to seek evidence of friendliness, but this is no reason to believe that the universe actually *is* friendly. We cannot simply assume that ethics is not incoherent.

> I am so far from feeling bound to believe for purposes of practice what I see no ground for holding as a speculative truth, that I cannot even conceive the state of mind which these words seem to describe, except as a momentary, half-willful irrationality, committed in a violent access of philosophic despair.
>
> (Sidgwick, *The Methods of Ethics*, 507)

5. *The sceptical solution.* Another alternative is to take the failure of ethics at face value. Ethics fails because it is incoherent. We should abandon the search for a unified account of rationality, admit that reason is an inadequate guide to action, and be guided instead by our instincts or desires. Some of Sidgwick's contemporaries did embrace the moral vacuum left by the collapse of traditional religion, as it allowed for a freer, more individualistic approach to life, especially in sexual morality. Sidgwick himself does seem to have favoured a more liberal approach to personal morality – though here, more than anywhere else, his public reticence makes it very difficult to discover what he actually thought. However, he regarded instinct and passion as very unreliable bases for a public morality. If scepticism became widespread, the result would be not liberation but chaos.

6. *The psychical solution.* His rejection of all these alternative solutions explains Sidgwick's enormous interest in psychic research. It is simply implausible that the interests of all individuals will completely coincide in the present life. Life after death is certainly not *sufficient* to solve the dualism of practical reason. The next world might be just as unfriendly as this world. However, life

after death is *necessary* for ethics. Unless there is another life where justice *might* be done, the attempt to systematize ethics is hopeless. The most urgent need for moral philosophers is to examine the evidence that human beings can survive death. Sidgwick's paranormal activities are thus not an eccentric sideline. They are central to his philosophical concerns.

Dissolving Sidgwick's dualism

The dualism of practical reason arises from four claims.

1. Egoism is rational.
2. Utilitarianism is rational.
3. The only way to reconcile two rational methods is to prove that they never conflict.
4. Utilitarianism and egoism conflict.

Modern philosophers have challenged each of these four claims. Perhaps the most obvious move, especially for utilitarians, is to deny that egoism is rational. Many of Sidgwick's earliest critics objected that his discussion of egoism is much less detailed, and less convincing, than his discussion of utilitarianism. Sidgwick justifies utilitarianism by showing how it underpins the principles of common-sense morality. Yet he freely admits that egoism conflicts with common-sense morality, and does not defend the rationality of egoism. Utilitarianism thus seems to have a much stronger case than egoism. If the two methods conflict, why not simply reject egoism?

Sidgwick replied to this criticism in later editions of his book. Part of his argument is negative. Utilitarians would only be justified in regarding egoism as irrational if they could show that egoism leads to utilitarianism – that it is logically inconsistent to accept egoism and not be a utilitarian. For instance, we might argue as follows. An egoist believes his own pleasure is good. Consistency requires that he recognize that everyone else's pleasure is equally a good. So the egoist's position is unstable, and the logical result is utilitarianism. Egoism is not rational, at least not when it conflicts with utilitarianism. (This argument is not explicitly presented by earlier utilitarians – as they did not share Sidgwick's worry about the threat of egoism. It rather represents the sort of thing a pre-Sidgwick utilitarian might have said if pressed on this point.)

Sidgwick rejects all such arguments. If someone is an egoist, we cannot rationally compel them to accept utilitarianism. At this point,

Sidgwick appeals to his hedonism. The notion of the general good is built on a more basic idea: that a particular state of consciousness is good for a particular person. The method that responds directly to the individual good is thus more basic than the method that responds to desirable consciousness in general. Egoism is more basic than utilitarianism, and utilitarians must admit that egoism is rational. (Sidgwick turns the proposed utilitarian argument on its head. We only feel a need to derive utilitarianism from egoism because we feel the prior claims of egoism. If the two conflict, we can thus offer no reason why egoism should give way.) In Sidgwick's defence, we could note that some form of egoism does have very strong intuitive appeal. The claim that it is rational for me to pursue my own interests is central to the very idea of rationality. Imagine a person who is completely indifferent to her own interests. Who would deny that such a person is irrational? (We return to the relationship between utilitarianism and egoism in Chapter 5.)

The second obvious response is to reject utilitarianism. Utilitarianism is infamously demanding – it leaves too little room for the agent's own interests. This is why it conflicts so sharply with egoism. A more plausible moral theory might not conflict with egoism. (This route naturally appeals to those who reject Sidgwick's claim that common-sense morality is equivalent to utilitarianism.) If we want a moral theory that does not conflict with egoism *at all*, then the obvious strategy is to derive that theory directly from egoism itself. If the requirements of morality *are* those of self-interest, there is no room for conflict. One recent example is the *contractarianism* of David Gauthier. Drawing on a tradition going back to Thomas Hobbes and John Locke in the seventeenth century, Gauthier identifies morality with the results of a bargain between rational self-interested agents who need a set of rules to govern their interactions with one another.

The reduction of morality to self-interest does not have broad appeal. Most people feel that it is morally heroic for someone to sacrifice his life to save others. But if morality *is* self-interest, then we must say either that such a person is immoral or that he is simply pursuing his own self-interest. The notion of morally admirable self-sacrifice would not make sense. Few moral theorists want to base their theory completely on egoism. Unless they do, however, they must admit some conflicts between morality and self-interest. They are then open to a variant of Sidgwick's original dualism, with utilitarianism replaced by morality in general. If egoism and morality are both rational, and if they conflict, then we must find some other way to reconcile them. (We could, of course, simply deny that morality is rational – perhaps it is irrational to be moral. Philosophers tend not to like this alternative. Even if morality is not rationally compulsory, philosophers do not want it to be irrational.)

Another approach is to make room for self-interest within morality, and *then* deny that egoism is rationally acceptable when it over-steps those limits. This is the approach of many theorists working in the utilitarian tradition. Some defend traditional utilitarianism – each person is allowed to give their own happiness only as much weight as the happiness of any other individual. Others construct versions of utilitarianism that allow agents to give disproportionate weight to their own interests, and then deny that it is rational to completely disregard the general interest when the two conflict. These utilitarians accept that, while utilitarianism and egoism represent different standpoints (the point of view of the individual and "the point of view of the universe" as Sidgwick put it), there is no reason why those two standpoints cannot be combined and reconciled within a single moderate moral theory. (We will explore these options further in Chapter 7.)

Drawing on themes from many of Sidgwick's contemporaries, such as Mill and Green, contemporary utilitarians also try to reduce the distance between utilitarianism and egoism by emphasizing the extent to which people's real interests do coincide. One strategy is to argue that the most valuable pleasures and achievements come from cooperative activities, where conflict is minimized. (We return to this strategy in Chapter 5.)

Many non-utilitarian philosophers see Sidgwick's dualism as an inevitable feature of his utilitarian framework. If we insist on seeing morality from the point of view of the universe, then we cannot expect to reconcile this with each person's view of their own life. Instead, we should see morality as a balance between the viewpoints of different individuals. To adopt the moral point of view is not to adopt some superhuman viewpoint, but merely to accept that my own self-interest must be constrained by the legitimate interests of others. One contemporary example is Thomas Scanlon's *contractualism*, where morality is based on rules that no one can reasonably reject. As we are balancing different viewpoints of the same type, it is much more reasonable to hope to reconcile them.

Another way to dissolve the dualism is to argue that, while utilitarianism and egoism are both rational, each has its own domain. Perhaps utilitarianism is the correct account of collective rationality, or of the "moral sphere", while egoism is the correct account of individual rationality. Or perhaps we should recognize that rationality (represented by egoism) and morality (represented by utilitarianism) are independent realms of practical thinking – each governed by its own laws, and neither subservient to the other. Perhaps, when Sidgwick asks for a single standard of rationality to resolve all disputes between the two realms, he is asking more of human reason than it can possibly hope to deliver.

Sidgwick's own favoured solution to the dualism of practical reason has not found many followers (if any) among contemporary moral philosophers. Contemporary utilitarians tend not to pay much attention to the possibility that we survive death, and probably none of them would accept that utilitarianism is incoherent if we do not survive. On the other hand, those philosophers who *do* take the possibility of another life seriously are almost always *not* utilitarians. Philosophers operating within a religious perspective typically emphasize strongly anti-utilitarian elements in their moral philosophy. Sidgwick's problem has been much more influential in recent moral thought than his solution. Despite its ultimate failure, Sidgwick's search for a coherent, intuitively appealing, rationally based moral theory sets the scene for modern moral philosophy.

This completes our survey of classical utilitarianism. We now begin the transition to modern utilitarianism, by exploring the different ways utilitarians have sought to justify their theory over the past two centuries.

Key points for the three classical utilitarians

Jeremy Bentham

- The utility principle tells legislators to produce laws that maximize happiness.
- The utility principle is the only possible basis for morality – anything else is merely "caprice".
- The utility principle should define all legal rights. The idea of natural rights is "nonsense on stilts".

John Stuart Mill

- "Actions are right in proportion as they tend to promote happiness, wrong as they tend to produce the reverse of happiness."
- Empiricism – all knowledge (including morality) is based on experience.

- The utility principle itself is derived from experience – especially from the fact that everyone desires happiness.
- The competent judge (who has experienced both) prefers higher pleasures to lower pleasures.
- Society can only interfere with an individual's liberty if his actions are a harm to others.
- The utility principle supports freedom of expression, democracy and rights for women.

Henry Sidgwick

- The dualism of practical reason:
  - There are two rational methods of decision-making: utilitarianism and egoism.
  - The two methods are irreconcilable.
  - Neither method is superior to the other.
  - Unless we can resolve this dualism, ethics is incoherent.

three

Proofs of utilitarianism

In this chapter, we examine how generations of utilitarians have sought to justify or prove their theory. For each proof of utilitarianism there are three questions to be asked.

1. What is being proved? (For instance, is utilitarianism offered as the best account of right action or of institutional justice?)
2. What are the competitors? (Utilitarianism is the best x – compared to what?)
3. What are the background philosophical and cultural ideas of what counts as an *adequate proof*?

The proofs of utilitarianism make much more sense if we take the trouble to answer these three questions. A decisive moment in the history of utilitarianism is Sidgwick's introduction of a *sceptical* option. This significantly raised the stakes for any proof. As well as showing that utilitarianism is the *best* available moral theory, we must now also prove it is *adequate* – as we can no longer assume that the best moral theory is adequate. We shall see that late twentieth-century moral philosophy brings us full circle, as the focus on intuitions allows us (once again) to content ourselves with discovering the best available moral theory.

In the nineteenth century, the battleground was typically between utilitarianism and non-utilitarian morality. We are offered a proof of utilitarianism in general – a justification of the utilitarian tradition as a whole. In the twentieth century, as moral philosophy becomes more professionalized, different forms of utilitarianism are often in competition with one another. A modern utilitarian often seeks to prove some particular form of utilitarianism, whose competitors include other forms of utilitarianism. (For instance, as we shall see in Chapter 6, contemporary rule-utilitarians seek to show that their theory is superior to act-utilitarianism.) As moral theories multiply, ever more sophisticated methods are needed to choose between them. This drives philosophers to construct ever more detailed and complicated counter-examples, as we shall see in subsequent chapters.

The present chapter thus acts as a bridge between our discussions of classical utilitarianism and of contemporary utilitarianism. In particular, by outlining the changing philosophical landscape, it helps us to see how (and why) the concerns, methods and questions of contemporary utilitarians differ from those of their nineteenth-century forebears.

Theological utilitarianism

We begin with one of the earliest utilitarian arguments. The object of proof is utilitarianism in general. Typically, theological utilitarians seek to show that standard moral rules can be given a utilitarian foundation based on the benevolence of God. Their alternatives include rules of conduct dictated by the church, and the direct revelation of divine commands. One purpose of utilitarianism is to provide a foundation for morality that bypasses the authority of particular church leaders. The philosophical and cultural context is definitely Christian, but strongly influenced by the Enlightenment. There is a strong emphasis on human reason, on the goodness of creation, and on the rational intelligibility of divine commands. Instead of relying on priests to tell us what God wants, we can use our knowledge of human nature, and of God's love for humanity, to deduce how God would want us to live.

Theological utilitarianism faces a number of problems. Some of these are general problems for any ethics based on religion. Is there a God? How do we know what God wants? If one task of morality is to enable us to live together despite our religious differences, then should not ethics be independent of divine revelation? Other problems are particular to theological utilitarianism. Is God a utilitarian? (The theological utilitarians were all Christians who believed that God is revealed in the Bible. The Bible attributes many specific moral judgements and acts to God. Some of these are hard to reconcile with utilitarianism.) How can we know whether God is a utilitarian without first deciding whether utilitarianism is the correct moral theory? If we have already chosen utilitarianism on other grounds, then what is the significance of appealing to the commands of God? This is a modern version of a problem first identified by Plato, and known as *Euthyphro's Dilemma* after one of the characters in Plato's dialogues. We all agree that the gods love what is good. But do they love it *because* it is good, or does the fact that they love it *make* it good? The first option requires some standard of goodness that is independent of the gods, while the second option makes goodness seem arbitrary.

Theological utilitarianism has few defenders among contemporary philosophers. Most Christian philosophers are strongly opposed to utilitarianism, while most utilitarians prefer a less religiously loaded foundation for morality. The main modern descendant of theological utilitarianism is *evolutionary utilitarianism*, which also seeks to derive morality from a tale about human origins. It argues that our moral beliefs, institutions and practices exist because they enabled our ancestors to survive and flourish. As utilitarians, we should obey customary morality, because it maximizes human happiness. Like theological utilitarianism, evolutionary utilitarianism faces two sets of objections. Some objections trouble any evolutionary ethic. How do we know what behaviour led to our ancestors' survival? Why should we equate ethics with survival? What if our ancestors survived because they were (say) genocidal or untrustworthy? Other objections apply especially to evolutionary *utilitarians*. Of particular concern is the fact that, while evolution may select patterns of behaviour that maximize survival and reproduction, there is no reason to believe that it favours the promotion of human happiness.

Bentham's proof

The object of Bentham's proof is utilitarianism in general. The crucial step is the claim that the only alternative to utilitarianism is *caprice* – a morality based on self-interest, passion or superstition. In particular, Bentham is attacking the status quo – morality based on the self-interest of the ruling class (especially lawyers, aristocrats and priests) and on religious superstition. Utilitarianism offers the only possible ultimate test for institutions, public codes of ethics or personal morality.

The context of Bentham's proof is philosophical radicalism. Human reason is needed to overthrow irrational tradition. Bentham's proof is radical in its rhetoric, even though his utilitarianism was often incremental and pragmatic on a day-to-day level. The rise of a literate class of people outside the establishment also provided an audience for Bentham's ideas, thus enabling him to present them in a non-technical, anti-establishment idiom.

From the perspective of contemporary philosophy, the main limitation of Bentham's proof is the subsequent development of alternatives he does not consider. Defenders of traditional morality, or of other non-utilitarian approaches to morality, might argue that it need not be based on caprice. Even within utilitarianism, theological and evolutionary utilitarians provide rational foundations for existing practices, and thus offer an alternative to Bentham's radical agenda.

A second problem, as many contemporary philosophers point out, is that establishing that morality must be responsive to human well-being is not sufficient to prove utilitarianism. A theory based on fairness, equality, freedom or natural rights might generate exactly the same objections to the status quo, whether in the eighteenth century or today. The abuses Bentham railed against would be contrary to almost any contemporary moral theory. You do not have to be a utilitarian to object to slavery or corruption. So Bentham cannot prove utilitarianism simply by pointing out that the status quo is not sufficiently responsive to human needs.

Even if Bentham did convince us to embrace utilitarianism in general, his proof cannot tell us what sort of utilitarians we should be. In particular, most of the questions addressed in later chapters of this book are left unanswered by Bentham's general proof.

Mill's proof

Mill defends utilitarianism as the ultimate standard of right and wrong. The alternative he has in mind is *intuitionism* – where moral truth is known directly via a special moral sense. The philosophical context is Mill's empiricist method and associationist psychology. Like all other knowledge, our knowledge of morality must be derived from observation. Pleasure and pain are the only relevant observable features, so they provide the only possible basis for morality. Recall the three key steps of Mill's proof.

1. The move from "people desire x" to "x is desirable".
2. The move from "the happiness of each person is good for him" to "the general happiness is a good for the aggregate of persons".

3. The claim that happiness is the *only* end: that everything we desire is either a *part* of happiness, or a *means* to happiness. (Without this step, we have not proved utilitarianism, but only the weak claim that happiness is one good thing – perhaps one among many.)

The most important part of Mill's proof, both for Mill himself and for subsequent critics, has been the final step. Having established that happiness is *a* desirable end, Mill now seeks to show that it is the *only* desirable end.

Mill's proof is inductive. He does not claim to prove that happiness is the only desirable thing. Rather, he claims that the only *evidence* we could possibly possess that something is desirable would be the fact that people generally desire it. Consider these two claims.

(A) *x* is desirable but no one desires *x*.
(B) *x* is not desirable even though people generally desire *x*.

Mill does not say that claims like (A) and (B) are self-contradictory. He says that it is never reasonable to believe such claims. Mill is not trying to provide a logical proof, but a *comparative* argument. Utilitarianism can give moral knowledge a more secure foundation than intuitionism.

It is vital to note that Mill is probably the last major philosopher, and certainly the last major utilitarian, for whom moral scepticism is not a serious worry. When he asks the question "What is desirable?", Mill does not consider the possible answer: "nothing". Nor does he consider this a credible answer to the question: "What *grounds* (or underpins or explains or justifies) morality?" Showing that utilitarianism fares better than its competitors is sufficient for Mill. This is not a peculiarity of Mill. It is a tendency he shared with most of his contemporaries – utilitarians and non-utilitarians alike. (Indeed, most of Mill's intuitionist opponents are much more hostile to scepticism than he is.) Many modern criticisms of Mill's proof, while they would be legitimate if aimed at a modern philosopher trying to use Mill's argument to defeat scepticism, are thus not really legitimate objections in Mill's own philosophical context.

Mill's proof does face some problems even in its own terms. Is happiness the only thing people generally desire? It is easy to construct a dilemma for Mill. If we *define* happiness in terms of desire, then Mill's claim is true, but only because it is circular and unhelpful. (The informative but controversial claim "People only desire happiness" becomes the trivial "People only desire what people desire".) On the other hand, if happiness is not defined in terms of desire, then Mill's claim seems obviously false. People desire quite a wide range of things other than their own happiness. Mill himself seems to admit this with his competent judge model of well-being. It is far from clear that people generally desire only what the competent judge would desire.

A second problem is that, like Bentham's, Mill's proof does not go far enough. There is a big step from the claim that only happiness is desirable to full utilitarianism. As we shall see in Chapter 7, modern utilitarianism combines a claim about what is desirable with a distinctive way to respond to desirable things. Utilitarians seek to *promote* or *maximize* value. (Mill himself might well endorse this further claim, but his proof does not establish it.) Non-utilitarians might agree that happiness is desirable, but conclude that, instead of becoming utilitarians, we should avoid making others unhappy or seek to make ourselves happy – we should respect or embody or express happiness rather than promoting it.

Overall, then, Mill's proof succeeds more in his terms than in ours, but is not entirely successful even in his own terms. For most modern utilitarians, it provides a clearly inadequate foundation for utilitarianism.

Sidgwick

Sidgwick's object of proof is universal benevolence. This is a more tightly defined form of utilitarianism than we find in either Bentham or Mill. Sidgwick's main alternatives are egoism, and various forms of dogmatic intuitionism. Sidgwick's crucial addition is to separate utilitarianism from egoism. This introduces *two* new alternatives: egoism itself, and scepticism motivated by the failure of reason to decide between utilitarianism and egoism.

Sidgwick's philosophical and cultural context has several elements. The most striking is an increase in academic rigour, due to the professionalization of philosophy. This goes along with the influence of Idealism – imported from the new German universities, and leading to a much more rigorous exploration of the foundations of morality. This exploration fed into a general climate of scepticism about traditional intellectual authorities – fuelled also by the Romantic critique of the Enlightenment faith in human reason, and by Darwin's critique of the biblical account of human origins.

Sidgwick offers only a partial proof of utilitarianism. This proof rests largely on what we today would regard as reflective equilibrium grounds (see pages 55–9). Sidgwick argues that utilitarianism implies the principles of common-sense morality. Sidgwick's proof is open to objections from two directions. Opponents of utilitarianism will deny that it coheres so well with common-sense morality, while defenders of utilitarianism will reject the dualism of practical reason, arguing that utilitarianism is superior to egoism.

We discussed Sidgwick's methodology in Chapter 2. Here are three general objections a modern non-utilitarian would make.

1. *Utilitarian intuitions.* Sidgwick's account of common-sense morality is largely based on his own intuitions. These are heavily influenced by utilitarianism. Contemporary non-utilitarian philosophers might be less happy with the moral principles that Sidgwick derives from utilitarianism. (One difference between Sidgwick and most modern reflective equilibrium theorists is that he acknowledges foundational intuitions – that egoism is rational and that utilitarianism is rational – which cannot be rejected in the search for an equilibrium.)

2. *Alternative foundations.* Sidgwick is too swift to conclude that utilitarianism implies the principles he discusses. This is a common objection to this particular method. Sidgwick's arguments might show that utilitarianism implies some principle regarding truth-telling or promise-keeping, but his evidence is insufficient to show that his utilitarian principles coincide precisely with those of common-sense morality.

3. *Too pessimistic.* Sidgwick's pessimism is also too swift. He ignores possible compromises between utilitarianism and egoism. In particular, because Sidgwick begins by unifying utilitarianism and common-sense morality, he overlooks the possibility that the principles of common-sense morality might yield neither utilitarianism or egoism, but rather a balance between the two. (We explore such attempts in Chapter 7.)

R. M. Hare's proof

After Sidgwick, there was not much original progress in philosophical discussion of utilitarianism until the 1960s. This may seem odd, as the intervening period saw great upheaval in the Western world, including the establishment of the welfare state – a project championed by early utilitarians such as Bentham and often defended in public on largely utilitarian grounds. Utilitarianism was eclipsed in professional philosophy at the very time it achieved dominance in public discourse. The reason for this was a philosophical climate unsympathetic to moral philosophy in general.

As a reaction to the perceived excesses of German Idealism and metaphysical speculation in the nineteenth century, English-speaking philosophers in the first half of the twentieth century adopted a modest view of the role of philosophy. Philosophy consists merely of linguistic analysis. Philosophers offer definitions of the meanings of words. The only philosophical job in morality would be the analysis of moral terms ("ought", "right", "wrong", "good", "evil", and so on). This attitude found its extreme expression in the work of the *logical positivists*, who privileged science and mathematics and sought a role for philosophy as a subsidiary to science. Substantive inquiry was the job of scientists, not philosophers. If substantive inquiry in metaphysics or morals or theology could not be made scientific, then it should not be undertaken at all.

When these philosophers did offer analyses of moral terms, these tended to be *deflationary*. Moral terms turned out to be either meaningless or mere expressions of the speaker's preferences or emotions. "*x* is wrong" simply meant "I do not like *x*" or "*x* – yuck!" The deflationary style of analysis was a common logical positivist move. It arose particularly in reaction to idealist metaphysics and traditional religion. Terms such as "the absolute" or "God" or "the soul" were rejected as meaningless because no analysis could enable them to be verified. The logical positivists offered, as an analysis of moral terms, the very option that Bentham had sought to avoid: morality became an expression of caprice. Substantive moral exploration would then be a job for psychologists, sociologists or economists, who all study people's actual preferences.

From the 1960s, the Oxford philosopher R. M. Hare offered a defence of utilitarianism from within this philosophical tradition. His first step is to reject the *emotivist* analysis of moral terms as expressions of emotion. He argues instead that moral terms are like commands or *prescriptions*. If I say "People ought not to murder", I am not expressing my emotions. Rather, I am issuing a command. It is as if I said: "Do not murder!" What distinguishes moral terms from other prescriptions is their universal character. With an ordinary command, I can tell you to do something without saying anything about what others should or should not do. A commanding officer who orders a particular soldier to advance is not committed to ordering everyone to advance. A moral term, by contrast, implies a *universal prescription*. If I am using the word in a moral sense, I cannot say that you ought not to murder without committing myself to the claim that, in the same circumstances, no one else should murder either. A moral statement, by definition, must be *universalizable*.

Hare's analysis thus explains why we have moral terms at all. This question was problematic for the emotivist. If moral terms are just expressions of emotion, why do we need them? After all, we have many other ways to express emotion. On Hare's view, moral terms have a unique grammatical role. They are our only terms for universal prescriptions.

The second half of Hare's proof aims to derive utilitarianism from universal prescriptivism. The key step is the move from universalizability to *impartiality* – the idea that the logic of morals must take equal account of everyone's preferences. The problem is that there is a logical gap between universalizability and impartiality. After all, as Sidgwick himself noted, a rational egoist might easily prescribe her own attitude universally – "Everyone should pursue (only) his or her own self-interest." Hare tries to bridge this gap in the following way. If I issue an ordinary command, then I do so on the basis of my own preferences. Of course, I could make a universal prescription based on my own preferences – "Everyone should do *x* because that is what I want". But no one would take any notice, because no one would regard such a prescription as *moral*. If I want you to take my universal prescription seriously, then I must base it, not only on my own current preferences, but also on the preferences I would have if I were you. I must *fully represent* to myself what it would be like to be in each person's situation. To make a moral claim, I must seek to reflect everyone's preferences impartially. And, Hare argues, the best way to do this is to ask myself what I would prefer if I (somehow) took on everyone else's preferences in addition to my own. I can only say "Everyone should do *x*", if *x* is what I would want if I had internalized all the preferences of everyone involved. What ought to be done is whatever maximizes total preferences. Impartiality thus leads directly to a form of utilitarianism based on a preference theory of well-being.

Like Sidgwick, and unlike Bentham or Mill, Hare is aware of the following range of shady characters who loom large in both contemporary philosophy and modern culture. Hare's primary aim is to defeat all of these characters. Because of his philosophical background, Hare's opponents are people who think that moral philosophy cannot be done at all, rather than moral philosophers who are not utilitarians.

Modern enemies of morality
The sceptic denies that we have reliable moral knowledge.
The nihilist denies there is any moral truth.
The amoralist is not motivated by morality.
The psychological egoist says we are only motivated by self-interest.
The ethical egoist says we should be only motivated by self-interest.

Hare's object of proof is *two-level* utilitarianism. At the *critical level*, where moral philosophers operate, he offers a comparatively pure form of preference-based utilitarianism. However, like many earlier utilitarians, Hare recognizes that pure utilitarianism is a very inadequate guide to life. We do better to live our everyday lives at the *intuitive level*, and rest content with generally reliable rules of conduct. The ultimate justification for these rules is that following them produces greater aggregate preference satisfaction than any other course of action.

Although Hare has various alternatives in mind, especially sceptical or nihilistic options, his actual method of proof does not introduce any particular alternatives. Hare does not even compare utilitarianism to other moral theories. This is because his method is logical deduction rather than comparison. He seeks to prove that utilitarianism is the *only possible* account of morality. If this proof succeeds, then it establishes utilitarianism over any *possible* moral theory. Any other moral theory *must* turn out to be either nonsense or identical to utilitarianism.

Hare's argument is thus very ambitious. There are two questions for any such argument. Are Hare's claims true? Even if they are true, is this entirely due to the meaning of moral terms, as Hare himself claims? We could answer "Yes" to the first question and "No" to the second. Or we might leave the first question unanswered, and then answer the second in the negative. This would be sufficient to undermine Hare's proof. Let us focus on the key notion of universalizability. Hare's use of this notion raises two particular questions.

1. *Are universalizability and impartiality necessary features of moral language?* Hare's claim is that moral language, by definition, must be both universalizable and perfectly impartial. Some contemporary moral philosophers deny this. They argue that a moral

system could be less than perfectly impartial. Instead of identifying the "moral point of view" with a perfectly impartial "point of view of the universe", we should regard it as a compromise between *my* point of view and those of other people. Hare must say, not just that such people are wrong, but that they do not even understand the meaning of moral terms. (We discuss these other theories in Chapter 7.)

2. *Is Hare's account of universalizability the correct one?* Hare assumes that, once we agree that moral language must be universal and impartial, we are led inexorably to utilitarianism. Yet many non-utilitarian moral philosophers are deeply committed to both universalizability and impartiality. In particular, moral philosophers influenced by Kant often build their moral theories on Kant's universalizability test: acceptable moral principles are those we can will as a universal law for all rational creatures. It is a striking feature of these moral theories that they are in sharp contrast to utilitarianism. Faced with this disagreement, why should we accept Hare's analysis of universalizability? Even if we do, why should we accept it *as a logical truth*? (We return to Kant's ethics in Chapter 7.)

General trends in recent moral philosophy have undermined Hare's proof. Many philosophers now reject the claim that philosophy must be limited to linguistic analysis. This is partly because linguistic analysis has not delivered as much as its proponents had claimed. Analysing the meaning of moral words cannot tell us anything about what we ought to do. Proponents of linguistic analysis conclude that we should reject moral philosophy. Most contemporary philosophers conclude instead that we should reject linguistic analysis. Or, at least, we should reject the idea that linguistic analysis exhausts philosophy. The failure of Hare's proof is thus less of a problem for modern moral philosophers than for Hare himself.

Reflective equilibrium: the modern style of proof

Today, most moral philosophers use a style of argument based on considered intuitions. The foremost exponent of this method was Rawls, who called it the *reflective equilibrium method*. The aim is to bring our considered judgements into an equilibrium – a coherent whole. The result is not a jumbled set of isolated intuitions, but a consistent moral world-view, where conflicts or inconsistencies between different moral intuitions or judgements are resolved by a process of reflection and argument.

Intuitions come in many degrees of abstraction. Some are judgements about particular cases, either actual or imaginary. For instance, we might judge that Bob should pay Mary the money he owes her, or that some particular response to a hypothetical situation would be wrong. Some intuitions are more general. For instance, we might begin with a commitment to the principle that people should keep their promises, or that a just society will ensure that everyone's basic needs are met. Intuitions can be even more abstract. Utilitarians often cite the intuitive appeal of one of the following principles.

1. *The reason to promote the good.* The fact that an action will promote human happiness gives us a reason to perform that action. If two actions will each promote human happiness, then we have reason to perform whichever one produces greater happiness. If we choose actions solely on the basis of the reason to promote the good, we will thus always opt for the action which maximizes happiness.
2. *The principle of harm prevention.* If we can prevent something bad from happening, without sacrificing anything of comparable moral importance, we ought to do so.
3. *The principle of aid to innocents.* If we are able to provide assistance to an innocent person in great need, at negligible cost to ourselves, then we ought to do so.
4. *The numbers do count.* If you must choose between the lives of one group of people and the lives of another group, you must choose the larger group.

These starting points are justified in a number of ways. Their proponents appeal to their intuitive plausibility, sketch arguments in their favour, point out that the principle is endorsed in some form by most non-utilitarian moral theories, or produce simple cases or thought experiments where the principle clearly applies. For instance, Shelly Kagan motivates the reason to promote the good by suggesting that only an extreme anti-utilitarian would deny that human happiness provides some reason for action. The reason to promote the good is thus common ground between the utilitarians and their more moderate opponents, who seek to combine it with other moral principles.

A classic example of the use of a thought experiment to motivate a utilitarian starting point is this tale from Peter Singer. Singer argues that you have a clear obligation to save the child. He concludes that there is a general duty to prevent harm.

The pond

You are walking to work in the morning when you pass a small child drowning in a pond. You are not in any way responsible for the child's predicament. You can save the child, at the cost of a wet suit and the loss of a few minutes. What should you do?

Utilitarian justification of the principle that numbers should count often appeals to tales such as the following. The utilitarian claims that it is clear that you should go to the first rock – saving five lives rather than one. The numbers do count. Only utilitarianism explains why.

The rocks

Six innocent swimmers have become trapped on two rocks by the incoming tide. Five of the swimmers are on one rock, while the last swimmer is on the second rock. Each swimmer will drown unless they are rescued. You are the sole lifeguard on duty. You have time to get to one rock in your patrol-boat and save everyone on it. Because of the distance between the rocks, and the speed of the tide, you cannot get to both rocks in time. What should you do?

Contemporary utilitarians typically argue that utilitarianism makes better sense of our considered moral judgements than any alternative. The object of proof is often some particular form of utilitarianism, such as rule-utilitarianism or act-utilitarianism. (For more on this distinction, see Chapter 6.) The reflective equilibrium method is also used to justify individual components of utilitarianism, as we shall see in our discussion of different accounts of well-being in Chapter 4. The overall aim is to justify the combination of a particular theory of well-being and a particular theory of right action.

In theory, the reflective equilibrium method aspires to a universal comparison. The conclusion is that some particular moral theory is better than any available alternative. In practice, reflective equilibrium theorists are typically more modest. Due to constraints of space and time, they often rest content with a comparison involving only two or three theories. For instance, many particular defences of rule-utilitarianism focus on demonstrating its superiority to act-utilitarianism or to some particular non-utilitarian alternative, such as

Kant's deontology or Aristotle's virtue ethics. (These alternatives are explored in Chapter 7.)

At other times, reflective equilibrium theorists discuss their preferred theory in isolation, without any explicit comparison at all. Instead, as a preliminary to demonstrating its superiority over other theories, they first try to show that their preferred theory does at least a reasonable job of bringing together our considered moral judgements. This technique is employed particularly in response to attempts, by *opponents* of some particular theory, to sidestep the full reflective equilibrium method in a different way. A complete demonstration that one theory does the best job of tying together our intuitions would be very difficult and time-consuming, as it involves balancing and bringing together all our moral principles and intuitions, and comparing what every possible theory says about them. It is hardly surprising that moral philosophers seek shortcuts. In particular, they seek *decisive intuitions*: "No acceptable moral theory can say x." For instance, any theory that permits the torturing of innocent children might be ruled out automatically. Once we have chosen a decisive intuition, we can use it to discredit a theory without engaging in a full reflective equilibrium comparison. If theory T says x, and if x violates a decisive intuition, then T cannot be acceptable. We thus have a knock-down objection to T. Chapter 5 explores some popular objections of this kind to utilitarianism. In the rest of this chapter, we explore the underlying methodological issues.

We begin with the easiest case. Suppose we have two theories: $T1$ and $T2$. $T1$ fails at least one knock-down test. It violates a decisive intuition. $T2$ passes all knock-down tests. It is consistent with all decisive intuitions. The reflective equilibrium method allows us to conclude that $T2$ is better than $T1$, at least until a further decisive intuition is uncovered.

We turn now to the harder (and much more common) case. Suppose we have many knock-down tests, many decisive intuitions. For every theory T, there is one x such that T implies x and x violates a decisive intuition. Recall that, under reflective equilibrium, our intuitions cover general principles as well as particular cases. Perhaps the only way a given moral theory can accommodate all our particular moral judgements is by violating some plausible general principle.

Alternatively, we may be unable to decide which intuitions are decisive. For instance, suppose someone is badly-off through no fault of mine, but I can assist them at no cost to myself. Everyone would agree, other things being equal, that it would be morally good for me to assist them. But am I *obliged* to do so? Utilitarians will say that I am. The fact that the person is in dire need gives me a morally relevant reason to assist them. If I can do so at no cost to myself, then I have no counter-vailing reason not to assist. Accordingly, I am obliged to do so. A *liber-tarian* moral philosopher would strongly disagree. They hold that all positive obligations must be voluntarily agreed to. However strong the other person's need, the fact that I am not responsible for it means that I cannot have any obligations to them.

It is hard to resolve this impasse philosophically. Utilitarians can say many things in favour of their intuition, but so can libertarians. It may be more productive to see the different intuitions as distinctive of two moral perspectives: utilitarian and libertarian. Such *distinguishing intuitions* are very useful when we are deciding which theory we prefer. But it seems question-begging to use them as knock-down objections to someone else's theory. Utilitarians can use their "decisive intuition" to explain why they are not libertarians, but they cannot expect liber-tarians to be convinced. Suppose we reach such an impasse. What should we conclude? There are several possible responses.

1. There is no adequate moral theory. If no theory accommodates all our intuitions, then all moral theories are inadequate. We should either be moral nihilists, or continue with morality in the absence of an adequate theory.
2. A moral theory can be adequate even though it fails some (seem-ingly) knock-down tests, and violates some (seemingly) decisive intuitions. This is because, as reflective equilibrium theorists, we are looking for the *best* moral theory. We may hope that the best theory will be completely intuitively satisfactory, but we cannot assume in advance that it will be.
3. Our search for an adequate moral theory is incomplete. If dif-ferent theories have different strengths and weaknesses, then perhaps we should seek a new moral theory that combines the strengths and avoids the weaknesses. Utilitarians argue that, given the strengths of utilitarianism, we should expect the new moral theory to be either a form of utilitarianism or (at least) a theory with considerable utilitarian elements.

The shift to the reflective equilibrium method explains why contem-porary utilitarians are so interested in accommodating our intuitions. Over the next two chapters, we explore some of the most difficult intui-tions for any utilitarian theory – those relating to happiness (Chapter 4) and injustice (Chapter 5).

Key points

- Proofs of utilitarianism are always influenced by background philosophical and cultural assumptions.
- A key turning point is Sidgwick's recognition of the threat of moral scepticism.
- Mid-twentieth-century utilitarians (such as Hare) sought logically watertight proofs, based on the meanings of moral terms.
- Late twentieth-century utilitarians (following Rawls' method) sought a reflective equilibrium – where all our considered intuitions fit together.

four

Well-being

Utilitarianism links morality to the maximization of human happiness. Two issues dominate modern utilitarianism. What *is* happiness? *How* is morality linked to happiness? The first question is the topic of this chapter.

The classical utilitarians were all, in different ways, hedonists. For them, happiness is pleasure (and the absence of pain). While hedonism still has its defenders, most modern utilitarians favour alternative views. This has led to a change in terminology. "Happiness" is thought to bias the discussion in favour of hedonism. Modern utilitarian philosophers talk in more neutral terms: *well-being, welfare, "whatever makes life worth living"*; while utilitarian economists tend to use Bentham's technical term *utility*.

We all think about well-being all the time. When we ask whether some particular experience will be good or bad; when you look back on your life and list the things that made it go well and those that made it go badly; when you compare the situations of two different people and ask who is better-off; when a friend seeks your advice on a major life choice, and you ask what would be better for her; when I look forward and ask whether my life will go better if I become a lawyer or a philosopher. Many things can make a life go better: pleasure, money, achievement, health, freedom. Many things can make a life go worse: pain, frustration, poverty, disappointment, grief. Some of these will be only *instrumentally* valuable – good only as a means to other ends. To take an obvious example, this is how most people feel about money. For philosophers, however, a theory of well-being should provide a list of *intrinsically* good things – the ends to which all other things are the means.

Modern utilitarians offer three broad accounts of well-being. This chapter briefly outlines the three theories, and asks how we might choose between them. (The separate question of how we might measure well-being is deferred until Chapter 8.)

1. *Mental state or experience views.* The only things intrinsically valuable are positive states of mind. The only intrinsic bads are undesirable states of mind. Nothing can improve the value of my life unless it affects how I feel, or what I experience. The classic example is *hedonism* – which evaluates experiences in terms of pleasure and pain.

2. *Preference or desire views.* The only thing that is valuable is to get what you *want, prefer* or *desire*. (Sometimes these different terms are used to mark subtle distinctions, but we can use them interchangeably.) A person's life goes well so long as their preferences are satisfied. Preference views often coincide with hedonism. Getting what you want will often give you pleasure, while not getting what you want often causes pain. However, the two can come apart if your preferences stretch beyond your own experiences, or if you prefer pain.

3. *Objective or substantive views.* Both mental state and preference views are *subjective*. What is good for me depends upon some particular fact about me – what gives me pleasure, or what I desire. The main alternative theory offers a list of things that are simply good for anyone, whether or not they want them or take pleasure in them. Such a list might include knowledge, achievement, living morally. (Most lists also include pleasure, the absence of pain, the satisfaction of desire, and personal autonomy – reducing the gap between objective and subjective theories.)

Hedonism

We begin with hedonism, the simplest and most popular mental state view. The claim that well-being is pleasure naturally raises three questions. What *is* pleasure? Is pleasure *always* good? Is pleasure the *only* good?

What is pleasure?

"Pleasure" is surprisingly difficult to define. How do you know if an experience is pleasurable? By examining a brain scan? By the feel of it? Or by consulting your preferences? Consider three basic views of pleasure.

1. *Physiological pleasure.* A particular organism's level of pleasure or pain is a natural fact, measurable in the normal scientific way – just as we might measure the weight of an animal, or the functioning of its digestive system. A scientist can tell if ice cream gives me pleasure by examining my brain.
2. *Phenomenological pleasure.* The value of an experience depends entirely on how it feels. Each experience has a *hedonic tone* or *intensity*, a level of felt pleasure or pain. These can be measured and compared. Ice cream is better for me than chocolate if and only if the pleasure of ice cream is more intense. (This refers only to the *intrinsic* value of ice cream pleasure. Ice cream might also have other, less desirable, indirect effects.)
3. *Preference.* The comparative values of two experiences depend upon the person's preferences. If I prefer the experience of ice cream to the experience of chocolate, then ice cream is more pleasurable.

These three accounts often go together. Compare an extreme pain with a very good pleasure. The pain involves physiological disruption and a negative hedonic tone, while the pleasure involves smooth physiological functioning and a positive tone. And I will certainly prefer the pleasure.

Unfortunately, the three definitions sometimes come apart. So we must choose between them. This illustrates a general technique of *analytic philosophy* – the style of philosophy adopted by most modern utilitarians. If we are studying a concept ("well-being", "pleasure"), we begin with a number of vague definitions (or "analyses"). We then seek *test cases* – real or imaginary situations where the definitions come apart. By examining test cases, we can decide which definition is correct.

Physiological definitions of pain do not always coincide with the feeling of pain. In physiological terms, people can die of pain even though they are unconscious and feel nothing. Some "anaesthetic" drugs leave the physiological basis of pain untouched, but remove the feeling of pain. People whose limbs have been amputated "feel" pain "in" their non-existent limbs. We should separate two questions. Are these unfelt events "pains"? Are they intrinsic bads? As moral philosophers, our interest is in the second question. We might need different definitions for other purposes. For medical or scientific purposes the physiological account may be best, as it groups together events with similar physiological causes and effects. But our focus is on human lives as they are lived. This is why most hedonists privilege phenomenology over physiology. If I do not feel or experience a "pleasure" or "pain", then it does not make my life go better or worse. (Of course, if the "unfelt pain" causes my death, then it is instrumentally bad for me. The question is whether the "pain" *itself* is a bad thing.) Suppose you went to the doctor feeling intense pain, and were told "there is nothing wrong with you". You might be relieved that you do not have (for instance) cancer. But would you conclude that you were not in pain?

If pleasure and pain were ordinary physiological properties, then we might hope to measure them objectively. The utilitarian calculus would then be easy. Once we move from physiology to phenomenology, however, there is no guarantee that the necessary calculations will be possible. Indeed, this is one reason for the demise of hedonism. (We return to the *measurement problem* in Chapter 8.)

Now compare phenomenological hedonism and preference hedonism. Patients given certain drugs, or undergoing certain brain operations, sometimes report that they feel pain but "no longer mind it". Some philosophers deny the possibility of "not minding a pain": it is part of the *definition* of pain that a painful experience is disliked. Even if we agree that it makes sense to talk of "a not-minded pain", the question still remains: is there anything wrong with such a pain? A preference hedonist says there is not, and thus that phenomenological hedonism must be mistaken. A phenomenological hedonist will reply that, if you do not mind the pain, then that must be because it does not have the intensity of *real pain*.

Many philosophers are reluctant to base definitions on bizarre or unusual situations. So here is a more ordinary case. People often deliberately opt for a less intense pleasure, or even a more intense pain. This is often for instrumental reasons. I choose orange juice over beer, even though beer is more pleasant, to avoid the negative experience of a hangover tomorrow. I go to the dentist today to avoid the (greater) pain of toothache tomorrow. However, not all such choices are instrumental. I may simply prefer the less intense experience. I choose to stay home reading rather than going to a dance party, even though I know the party would produce more intense pleasure. Phenomenological hedonism suggests I have made a mistake – the more intense pleasure would be better for me. Preference hedonism can avoid this result: the better pleasure is whichever one I prefer. However, as we saw in our discussion of Mill's competent judge, preference hedonism puts us on a slippery slope. If we judge pleasures by preferences, what do we do if people prefer things other than pleasure? This leads us to the two main objections to hedonism.

Is pleasure always good?

Some pleasures seem morally wrong. This gives rise to one of the most famous objections to utilitarianism.

Christians and lions

You are the ancient Roman official responsible for entertainment at the Colosseum. There is a full house. The crowd is uninterested in chariot races, or athletics, or even gladiatorial contests. What would give them most pleasure is to see a small group of Christians eaten alive by hungry lions. Utilitarianism says you should feed the Christians to the lions, as their suffering is outweighed by the pleasure of many thousands of spectators.

Suppose you believe that you should not feed the Christians to the lions. Can you still be a hedonist? Your first step is to separate hedonism from utilitarianism. Hedonism, on its own, is just a theory of well-being. It tells us what is good for each person – it does not tell us how to act. A hedonist who is not a utilitarian can avoid sacrificing the Christians – perhaps because it is always wrong to torture innocent people. (As we shall see in Chapter 5, utilitarians who are not hedonists face very similar objections – which does suggest that this is a general problem for utilitarianism, not one specific to hedonism.)

So hedonists could avoid sacrificing the Christians. But suppose the Christians are fed to the lions anyway – and the spectators enjoy sadistic pleasure. Does hedonism have to say this pleasure *is good for the spectators*, as it makes their lives go better? Some hedonists accept this conclusion. Many bad things happen in this tale. It is bad, *all things considered*, that the Christians are tortured. (It is certainly bad *for the*

Christians.) Sadistic pleasure is *instrumentally bad* – as it encourages people to commit or support torture. For the same reason, it is bad that the world contains people who get pleasure from torture rather than tiddlywinks. But – *considered in isolation* – the sadistic pleasure itself is *good*. A world where Christians are tortured and sadistic pleasure is felt is better than an (otherwise identical) world where Christians are tortured and sadistic pleasure is not felt.

Many people find this hard to accept. If you take pleasure in the torture of others, then this makes your life go *worse*, not better. It is not that the value of sadistic pleasure is *outweighed* by other factors – sadistic pleasure has no value *at all*. Suppose one of the spectators is your best friend, and you want her life to go as well as possible. You know she enjoys a good lion feeding. Would you advise her to go to the Colosseum? Would it do her good?

A good test case is *virtual torture*. Suppose the spectators are in a virtual reality game. No one is actually tortured – there is only sadistic pleasure. Is this game – *in itself* – a good or bad thing? Suppose the spectators *know* the torture is not real. Does that make their pleasure more respectable?

These simple tales illustrate the complexities of hedonism. They also illustrate the problems facing our two remaining definitions of pleasure. Phenomenological hedonists have difficulty avoiding the dubious claim that sadistic pleasure is a benefit to the person who experiences it – if it *feels* good, how can it not *be* good? Preference hedonists cannot avoid this claim either, as our imaginary spectators prefer sadistic pleasure to harmless pleasure.

Is pleasure the only good?

Recall the following objection from our discussion of Mill.

The pig philosophy objection
Polly has two choices: a life filled only with intense pig pleasures, or a successful human life as a philosopher with less intense human pleasures. Hedonism must tell Polly to choose the pig life, as the pleasures are more intense. This is good advice if Polly is a pig, but not if Polly is a human being.

A related dilemma arises when we focus on the *number* of pleasures rather than their intensity.

> **Haydn and the oyster**
> The good fairy offers Ollie Haydn two choices. He can live a flourishing successful human life for 100 years (like his father the famous composer), or live as a happy oyster experiencing very simple pleasures. The oyster life can be as long as Ollie wants – even up to millions of years. Each year of oyster life is valuable. Even if this value is very slight, it is not zero. However much value we assign to a flourishing human life, this can be outweighed by a sufficiently enormous number of oyster years. If Ollie is a hedonist, he must choose the oyster life.   (Adapted from Crisp, *Mill on Utilitarianism*, 24)

Opponents of hedonism object that a flourishing human life is more valuable than any oyster life, no matter how long. Can hedonism accommodate this result? Phenomenological hedonism seems stuck. In terms of intensity and quantity, both the pig and oyster lives contain more felt pleasure than the philosopher's life. Preference hedonism fares better. If you prefer the philosopher's life to either the pig or oyster life, then it is more pleasurable. But what if, ignorant of the richness of philosophy, you prefer the other life? Does that make it more pleasurable?

As we saw in Chapter 2, Mill uses a preference view to avoid the objection that hedonism is a philosophy of pigs. Pig (lower) pleasures are less *desirable* than human (higher) pleasures. Even if pig pleasures are more intense, any *competent judge* would prefer the human pleasures. Similarly, anyone who properly understands the nature of human pleasures and oyster pleasures will prefer the human life to any oyster life, even an eternal one. And no competent judge will prefer sadistic pleasures.

At this point, preference hedonism faces two main problems: disagreement between competent judges and preferences beyond pleasure.

1. *Disagreement between judges.* The preference hedonist faces a dilemma. Either competent judges disagree, or they do not. If competent judges disagree, then the obvious solution is to go with the majority. (Indeed, this seems the only principled solution.) But what if I am a competent judge in a minority? I have experienced both pleasures, but I happen to prefer the pleasure of mud-eating, pushpin, *Time Cop* over ice cream, cricket, philosophy, *The English Patient*. Does this mean that my preferences are mistaken, even though I am a competent judge?

The alternative is to deny that competent judges disagree. Everyone who has *truly appreciated* both pleasures prefers philosophy to pushpin – everyone prefers the full human life to the oyster life. But now hedonism threatens to become circular (or "true by definition"). How do we know if someone has truly appreciated philosophy? Because they prefer it to pushpin. How do we know that someone has learnt to appreciate art movies? Because they prefer them to action movies. It looks as if we independently decide that art movies are better than action movies, and then use this judgement to decide who is a competent judge. The actual preferences of the competent judge are then "a loose wheel" – we do not learn anything by observing what the competent judge prefers. All the work is done by our definition of competence.

2. *Preferences beyond pleasure.* The competent judge test highlights a deeper problem for all hedonists. Suppose all competent judges agree. They all prefer reading philosophy to playing pushpin. The preference hedonist concludes that the *experience* of reading philosophy is better, according to these judges, than the *experience* of playing pushpin. Philosophy gives *more pleasure* than pushpin.

This inference is illegitimate. What competent judges choose is the *activity* of philosophy. They may do this because they value knowledge (for instance) more than pleasure. Their preference for philosophy does not tell us their views about the pleasure or experience of philosophy. And, if we were to seek those views, we might find that they value some things more than pleasure. (This was the point of Carlyle's original objection to utilitarianism.) To prove that people do not just value experiences, Robert Nozick presents a striking tale.

Nozick's experience machine

Ella has two options. She can live the rest of her life in the ordinary world, or she can be plugged into an experience machine. Once inside the machine, she will forget she is in it. Electrodes attached to her brain will give her exactly the same experiences as in the real world, except that her life will be more pleasant. She will be happier, prettier, healthier, wealthier, more successful – with more friends and less suffering in her life. What should Ella do?

The fact that it is more pleasant gives Ella a reason to choose the experience machine. And hedonism says that Ella has *no possible* reason *not* to choose the experience machine – there is nothing wrong with her experiences. So she must plug herself in. Nozick presents this tale as a knock-down objection to hedonism. His argument is simple.

1. Life in the experience machine lacks something valuable.
2. Hedonism says that life in the experience machine lacks nothing valuable.
3. Therefore, hedonism is false.

The experience machine is a very useful test case. If you would not choose life in the machine, then you are not a hedonist. If it is rational to decline the machine, then it is rational to reject hedonism. If it is irrational to choose the machine, then hedonism is definitely wrong.

To imagine the experience machine, we must put aside all practical difficulties. Ella is not worried that the experience machine will malfunction, that it might be reprogrammed by political extremists who will give her a very undesirable kind of life, or that her experiences in the machine will be unrealistic. (Most people would not want to spend their life in a game of space invaders, or a very badly designed reality television show.) Hedonists can then argue that Nozick's aversion to the experience machine is actually based (perhaps unconsciously) on these practical difficulties. If we really were confident that the experience machine would work, then we would choose it.

I have discussed this example with many philosophy students (and others) over the years. In my experience, people divide pretty much down the middle – about half would choose the experience machine, while half would not. This might suggest that people are equally divided between hedonism and non-hedonism. However, we need to be careful. A hedonist *would* choose the machine. But a non-hedonist *might also* choose it. If you would not choose the machine, you're not a hedonist. But if you would choose it, this does not show that you *are* a hedonist. Your well-being might just happen to coincide with hedonism in this particular case. (As we shall see, this is exactly what the opponents of hedonism argue.)

Suppose you agree with Nozick. Even with proofs of reliability, testimonials from satisfied customers, and a government guarantee that the machine is terrorist-proof, you still think Ella should decline the experience machine. Why might she do this? What is missing? Nozick's answer is that people want to actually *do* things, not merely to *have* experiences. Suppose Ed's life ambition is to climb Mount Everest. After years of training, involving considerable sacrifice, Ed arrives at the base camp in the Himalayas, where he is approached by an experience machine operator. The operator offers Ed the experience of climbing Mount Everest. "After all", says the operator, "you came here for this experience, and I can give it to you risk-free."

Ed declines. He does not just want to feel *as if* he is climbing Mount Everest; he actually wants to climb it. He wants the actual achievement, not merely the delusion of achievement. This is not an uncommon reaction. Suppose the operator takes his machine to the Olympic Games, and offers all competitors the experience of winning a gold medal. "You have trained for four years to get this experience, and I can guarantee it." (This would maximize well-being, as everyone would experience the pleasures of winning, and all the side-effects of winning – fame, adulation, a career on the talk-show circuit, relationships with other celebrities, and so on.)

Perhaps some competitors would accept. But most would reply that they want *to win*, not merely to think they have won, or to have the feeling of winning. Think of our reaction to movies or stories where someone wakes up one morning and discovers that their whole life has been a lie (*The Truman Show, The Matrix*). Suppose you woke up tomorrow and discovered that you had spent the last ten years on a reality television programme. (You'd always wondered why your parents were so keen to send you to boarding school in Swaziland.) The people you thought were your friends are actually actors who have never liked you. Obviously, you would be upset. Nozick argues that you would also re-evaluate the last ten years of your life. You thought your life was going very well, and you have discovered that it was not. The hedonist must deny this. Whatever its source, the pleasure you experienced was real. Your discovery cannot make your previous life less valuable than you thought it was.

Suppose you accept that something *is* missing in the experience machine. By definition, there is nothing wrong with your experiences in the machine. So the missing element concerns the way your experiences relate to reality. Philosophers offer three explanations. A hedonist might reply that the right relationship to reality is part of what makes *pleasures* valuable. Competent judges prefer real life to experience machine life. So real life is more pleasurable. However, most people think this move abandons the basic hedonist premise that the value of my life is entirely a function of how my life feels, or seems, *to me*.

At the other end of the spectrum, *objectivists* argue that an appropriate connection to reality is intrinsically valuable. A life of delusion or deception is not a good life. It is always irrational to plug into the experience machine – so long as life in the real world is not too awful. (For instance, Ella might plug in if she has a painful terminal illness that can only be cured by the experience machine.)

Preference theorists take a middle road. There is no universal answer to the experience machine. Some people are better-off in the machine, others are worse-off – even though everyone has the same quality of experience. What really matters is getting what you want. Some people *want* a strong connection to reality, while others do not. Some people want genuine achievement, while others value only the experience. The preference theory thus explains *all* reactions to the experience machine. Some people choose the machine because they prefer pleasure. Those people should enter the machine, not because pleasure is intrinsically good, but because they prefer it.

The preference theory

All utilitarians are interested in preferences or desires. Well-being is intimately related to getting what we want. For the hedonist, however, a person's preferences are only an *indicator* of well-being. Giving someone what they want is often the most reliable way of giving them pleasure – and thereby making them better-off. Even on the preference-based view of pleasure, preferences only determine which experiences count as pleasures. It is still the pleasurable experience itself that is intrinsically valuable. (This is clear with Mill himself. His competent judge does not *make* certain pleasures valuable, he merely *guides* us to the best pleasures.) For the preference theory, by contrast, preference is *constitutive of* well-being. Giving someone what they want *is* making them better-off. Something is good for you if and only if it satisfies one of your *intrinsic preferences*. (That is, you want it for itself, not merely as a means to something else.) It is good for me to get ice cream if I want ice cream, but not otherwise.

The preference theory is related to Mill's notion of the competent judge, but there are two key differences. As we have just seen, instead of using preferences to test the value of pleasures, we now use preferences directly as the *criterion* of well-being itself. Furthermore, Mill seems to suggest the preferences of competent judges will produce a ranking of pleasures that holds true for everyone. The preference theory, at least in its initial formulation, rejects this potentially paternalistic move. Your well-being is constituted by *your* preferences, not someone else's.

These features of the preference theory give it several advantages over hedonism: a greater connection to reality, a reduced risk of paternalism, and a greater amenability to measurement.

The preference theory easily accommodates a Nozickean dissatisfaction with the experience machine. It also accommodates the opposite view – that the experience machine is harmless. Indeed, the preference theory offers an *explanation* of this disagreement. It is good for Ella to avoid the experience machine, *if* she wants a life connected to reality. But if she lacked this preference, then the experience machine would be equally good, or perhaps better. The machine is very bad for those who prefer a strong connection to reality, but it may be good for others.

Many people are very anxious to avoid "paternalism" – the presumption that I know what is good for you better than you do. A theory of well-being can seem paternalistic if it implies that people are not the best judges of what is good for them. The preference theory is designed to avoid paternalism. A devout hedonist would *force* people into the experience machine to make their lives go better against their will, whereas a preference theorist would leave each person to choose for themselves. Hedonists will deny that their theory is paternalistic in practice, as we invariably promote pleasure best by leaving people free to choose for themselves. But the preference theory seeks a more principled response to paternalism – one that does not depend upon a calculation of probabilities.

Pleasure is very difficult to measure. How can we compare your pleasure eating ice cream with your pleasure going to the movies? How can we compare my pleasure with yours? By contrast, preferences are easy to measure, because they are *revealed* in action. If I offer you a choice between ice cream and the movies, I can observe your preference. You will choose what you prefer. If I offer two people a chance to purchase ice cream, then the one who offers more money reveals a stronger preference.

This advantage is especially significant if we apply utilitarianism to large institutions. We cannot design institutions to maximize total pleasure. But we can maximize preference satisfaction by designing institutions where people are free to choose. Even if we cannot calculate the *amount* of preference satisfaction we produce, we know we have maximized preference satisfaction if everyone is free to follow their own preference. (We return to these issues in Chapter 8.)

Some of the most exciting work in contemporary utilitarianism is at the intersection of economics and philosophy. Because they focus on measurement and institutional design, economists have different preoccupations from philosophers. Economists want a workable proxy for well-being, while philosophers seek a watertight definition. Revealed preferences are the basis of modern economics, as they are thought to be the most reliable indicator of well-being, especially when we are evaluating institutions. A major challenge in contemporary economics is to design institutions where everyone has a genuinely equal chance to reveal their preferences. This is especially significant in development economics – the economics of poor people and poor nations – where many factors may interfere with the free expression of preferences, such as deficiencies in political power, freedom of expression, literacy, nutrition and basic health.

Is preference sufficient?

The preference theory raises many questions. We focus on three.

1. Do all desires count?
2. Must we know that our desires are satisfied?
3. How do we count desires?

The preference theory consists of two related claims. The first is that preference satisfaction is *sufficient* for well-being: if I know that *x* satisfies one of your intrinsic preferences, then I know *x* will be a benefit to you. (Of course, satisfying a preference can be *instrumentally* bad for you, for instance if you have a very bad allergic reaction. But the preference satisfaction *in itself* is always a benefit.) The second claim is that preference satisfaction is *necessary* for well-being: nothing can be a benefit to anyone unless they prefer it. If I know that you do not prefer *x*, then I know that *x* is not intrinsically a benefit to you.

Most objections to the preference theory focus on the first of these two claims. (We return to the second in our discussion of the objective list theory.) They deny that preference satisfaction is sufficient for well-being, by imagining cases where satisfaction of a preference does not benefit the person. People can want, desire or prefer pretty much anything. Some preferences seem bad for the person, or at best worthless. More strikingly, other preferences reach far beyond the person's own life. The astronomer Carl Sagan wanted there to be intelligent life on other planets. Leonardo da Vinci hoped that one day human beings would fly. If you see a famine on the television news, you may wish that those people will be spared. In an airport lounge, you meet a stranger with a potentially life-threatening illness. You want him to recover, even though you know you will never know whether he did. Suppose you have all these preferences and each is satisfied. There is life on other planets, human beings do fly, the famine is averted, the stranger lives.

Does the simple fact that the preference was satisfied benefit *you*? Opponents of the preference theory argue that it does not, as the *content* of these preferences is too remote from your life. Such distant events have nothing to do with you.

Suppose we want to rule out these irrelevant desires. One common first move is a restriction to "I-desires": preferences that directly relate to the person's own life. Your life goes better if your preference for eating ice cream is satisfied, but not if there is life in distant galaxies. The first preference relates to yourself, while the second does not. A good life is one where all your *intrinsic I-desires* are satisfied – you get the things you want in themselves *for yourself*.

Suppose we agree that *only* I-desires contribute to a person's well-being. Do *all* I-desires count? Consider a new tale where you clearly satisfy an I-desire but seem to make the person worse-off. You are hosting a party for four friends. Bob wants to drink the liquid in your glass, thinking it is beer. You give Bob the glass, even though you know it contains orange juice, to which Bob is allergic. Bob satisfies his desire, and is horribly ill. When she arrives at the party, Mary gives you her car keys, telling you not to return them to her if she is drunk. Two hours later, Mary expresses a desire to have her keys. You return them to her, even though you know she is very drunk. As the party wears on, you give heroin to Albert, who is an addict. Finally, your friend Jenny has given you the key to her medicine cupboard, telling you not to return it if she is depressed. When Jenny asks for the key at the end of the party, you return it, even though you know Jenny usually gets depressed after a night out and might well kill herself.

Do you make each person's life go better by giving them what they want? Most people would say "No". How might the preference theorist reply? One response is to distinguish between a benefit *considered in isolation* and a benefit *all things considered*. The preference theorist could agree that you do not make the person's life go better overall. But this is because, in each case, *other* preferences conflict with the preference you satisfy. Bob does not desire orange juice or illness. His overall level of preference satisfaction is higher if he does not drink the juice. In her sober state, Mary values her (sober) desire not to drive drunk more than her subsequent desire (when drunk) to drive. As Mary is best placed to compare her own preferences, you should not return the keys. Although Albert desires heroin, he also desires not to be addicted to heroin. And the latter desire is more important to him. (In technical terms, philosophers say that Albert's *second-order desires* – what he wants to want – are out of kilter with his *first-order desires* – what he does want. And, in such a case, the second-order desires are more representative of the person's true interests.) Jenny's strongest considered desire is to stay alive. You do not maximize her *overall* preference satisfaction by enabling her to kill herself. You do each of your friends *some* good by satisfying their preference, but this good is outweighed by the preferences you thwart.

This move is similar to the hedonist defence of sadistic pleasure – it is bad overall, but intrinsically good. As with sadistic pleasure, many people are not satisfied with this response. They argue that these preferences should not count at all. If we agree, we must place further conditions on a person's preferences. Two possibilities are a *full information requirement* (for instance, Bob's desire for the juice does not count because he lacks crucial information) and a *prudence requirement* (for instance, Mary's desire to drive while drunk should not count, because it is not consistent with her own considered view of her long-term best interests). The challenge for any such test is to avoid circularity. (Question: which desires enhance well-being? Answer: those that a fully informed prudent person would have. Question: what desires would a fully informed prudent person have? Answer: those that enhance well-being.)

Even when a desire is not harmful, it can seem pointless – especially compared to more important desires. Contrast a desire to count all the blades of grass in the park with a desire to prove a complicated and important mathematical theorem, or to find a cure for cancer. We might say either that the desire to count blades of grass is *worthless*, or merely that it is *worth less* than the desire to cure cancer. In both cases, something is valuable beyond the fact of my preference and the strength of that preference. This points us beyond the preference theory.

Posthumous harms

Events after a person's death can certainly affect how we think about the person's life, as shown in the following examples. Derek devotes his whole life to preserving the monuments of Venice. The day after he dies they are destroyed by terrorists. Ally devotes her life to providing her children with a good start in life. The day after she dies they are wiped out by the plague. Tony spends his entire life defending his own reputation for personal integrity. The day after he dies his reputation is destroyed by the publication of his spin doctor's diary. Given the significance these projects played in each person's life, does not their posthumous failure retrospectively reduce the value of their lives?

Post-mortem events can also *improve* a person's life. Consider the contrast between Lex and Leia – two scientists who are equally well regarded in their lifetime. Lex spends his entire life arguing that life on earth came from the planet Krypton. Lex's theory attracts attention in his lifetime. But soon after his death scientists discover there is no planet Krypton, and Lex is forgotten. Leia devotes her entire life to the theory that life on earth evolved from gum-wrappers discarded by untidy space tourists from the planet Alderon. Leia's theory provides the foundation for a complete revolution in science. Generations of scientists pore over Leia's work and hail her as a genius. Leia is a more successful scientist than Lex. They both desired to produce an influential and enduring scientific theory. Leia's preference is satisfied, while Lex's is not. It seems natural to say that Lex's life was wasted, while Leia's was not.

Posthumous events can be relevant to a person's life. But can they affect her *well-being* – how well her life goes? Can there be posthumous harms or benefits? On the preference theory, as we have interpreted it so far, posthumous harms and benefits will be commonplace, as many desires are only satisfied after the person's death. Many of these (such as Leonardo's desire that human beings fly) are ruled out by our earlier restriction to I-desires. But some I-desires are also satisfied only posthumously, as when a parent's desire that her children graduate from high school is only satisfied after her tragically early death. In this case the desire is only *contingently posthumous*, as this person's children could have graduated during her lifetime had she lived longer. But other desires are *intrinsically posthumous*. If I want to be remembered after my death, then my desire cannot possibly be satisfied while I am alive. (I could, of course, fake my own death to find out what people will say when *they think* I am dead, but this is not the same thing.) Many other desires, even though logically they *could* be satisfied before death, are almost certain to be satisfied only posthumously. Charlotte hopes that her great-great-great grandchildren will continue her support for utilitarianism, even though (like most modern utilitarians) she does not think she will exist when this happens. If my well-being is increased whenever one of my desires is satisfied, then post-mortem events will often improve (or reduce) the quality of my life.

The question of posthumous benefits provides a good case study of the way moral philosophers attempt to construct theories using our everyday judgements and intuitions. Some people find the very idea of posthumous benefits or harms unintelligible. Once a person's life is ended, nothing can make it go better or worse. These people will regard the fact that it admits widespread posthumous benefits as a *reductio ad absurdum* of the preference theory – a result so absurd that it invalidates the whole approach. Surely the quality of my life can only depend on events within my life. If we allow posthumous benefits or harms, then we can never say how good a person's life has been. No matter how long ago she died, there is always the chance that some new event will upset our calculations.

Many preference theorists would be happy to rule out posthumous desires. Unfortunately, it is very difficult to stop there. We appear to be on a slippery slope towards the conclusion that there are no harms or benefits that do not directly impinge on the person's consciousness. To illustrate this, suppose Mary and her partner are both injured in a car crash and taken to separate hospital wards. Mary's dying wish is that her partner survive. Her partner dies just *before* Mary, but Mary never knows. Can we allow this to affect Mary's well-being? It looks as if we can, as the event occurs during Mary's lifetime, and satisfies one of her preferences. Sadly, things are not so simple. If we do not believe in posthumous harms, then we must conclude that, if the partner's death had occurred a few moments later, then this event would not have affected Mary's well-being. But it seems ridiculous for a delay of a few moments to make such a big difference. To make the issue more vivid, suppose you want to know how well Mary's life went, but you do not know the relative times of the two deaths. Would you need to find out who died first? It seems unlikely that you would. If events during Mary's life can reduce its value even though she is never aware of them, it is arbitrary to say that events after her death cannot. If we reject posthumous harms, then consistency requires that we refuse to allow her partner's death to affect Mary's well-being at all, even if that death occurs during her life.

If we reject posthumous harms, then it looks as if we must also reject all desires whose satisfaction does not impact on the person's life. Things would obviously be different if Mary became aware of her partner's death before her own death – as she would suffer and she would know that her preference had not been satisfied. So perhaps desires should only count if the person is aware that they have been satisfied. We should add an *experience requirement* to our preference theory of well-being. Nothing benefits me unless I am aware of it.

To allow us to formulate this new version of the preference theory precisely, some utilitarians distinguish two ways a desire can be satisfied, which we might label *fulfilment* and *satisfaction*. My preference is fulfilled so long as whatever I want happens. It is only satisfied if

I am aware of this. Once we have made this distinction, we see that some of our earlier cases of "satisfied preferences" really involved only fulfilment. Leonardo's preference that human beings fly was fulfilled, but it was not satisfied. If nothing benefits me unless I am aware of it, then only a satisfied preference is a benefit.

Although we need it to avoid posthumous harms, the experience requirement has hidden costs of its own. Recall that one motive for the preference theory is to accommodate Nozick's rejection of the experience machine. If I want my experiences to be real, then my life goes worse if they are not real, *even if* I never discover this. If I want to have genuine friends and to be well-regarded, then my life goes badly if I am not well-regarded and have no genuine friends, even if I never discover the truth. The experience requirement thus seems to undermine one key advantage of the preference view over hedonism, as it eliminates the possibility of benefit (or harm) without knowledge.

We began with an intuitive objection to posthumous harms. When combined with Nozick's intuitive reaction to the experience machine, this objection leads us to an *inconsistent triad*. We have three incompatible claims, each of which seems intuitively compelling.

1. We must avoid having to accept that posthumous harms exist.
2. If we are to avoid having to accept that posthumous harms exist, then we cannot object to the experience machine.
3. We must reject the experience machine.

Obviously, we must abandon one of these three beliefs. At this point, people's intuitions diverge. Some people may feel we went wrong at the very start. Perhaps we should simply accept posthumous harms and benefits, and thus easily avoid the experience requirement. If a person devotes her entire life to a central project – sacrificing everything else in its pursuit – then it does seem plausible that her well-being is tied up in the success of that project. If you were offered a choice between Leia's life and Lex's, would you really be indifferent – as the experience requirement suggests? Or would you prefer Leia's? This position is perhaps most plausible in the case of harms. If a person's project collapses after his death, then this might render his life meaningless. Would you choose Derek's or Tony's life over a less tragic alternative?

Before we accept posthumous harms, we need to consider another general problem they highlight for the preference theory. We can introduce this by noting that the puzzle of posthumous desires arises only if either death ends your *existence* (as most contemporary utilitarians believe), or (for some other reason) events after a person's death cannot affect the value of their *earthly* life. If people continue to exist after their earthly death – whether in heaven or through reincarnation – then post-mortem harms or benefits are philosophically unproblematic. It will be difficult for us to know what those harms and benefits will be, but such is life.

Our new problem arises if we assume that death involves the disappearance of my present desires. This obviously happens if death is non-existence. If I no longer exist, then my preferences no longer exist. But even if I continue to exist after my death, I will probably lose most of my earthly desires. Therefore, if the posthumous fulfilment of my preferences can improve my life, then it must be possible for the fulfilment of a preference to be a benefit even when that preference no longer exists. But this general principle has some odd implications, as the following tale illustrates.

The late gift
When he is six, Bruce tells Alfred he wants to own a bat costume. Thinking Bruce is not ready for such a responsibility, Alfred waits until Bruce is twenty-one, and then gives him a bat costume. Bruce, having completely forgotten his early desire, is unimpressed. "What do you think I am – six?"

Alfred's gift fulfils a preference Bruce once had. We might even say that the gift *satisfies* Bruce's preference, especially if Bruce is aware that he is getting something he once wanted. But does Alfred benefit Bruce? The puzzling nature of the suggestion that Alfred does benefit Bruce is even clearer in a first-person story. Suppose that, instead of buying the costume, Alfred merely reminds Bruce of his earlier desire. Should Bruce buy himself a bat costume (rather than a new suit) simply because he wanted one when he was six?

The challenge is to keep posthumous harms without admitting the universal significance of abandoned desires. One solution is to count only the person's *stable adult* desires. If you keep changing your mind, then we have no good reason to fulfil the particular preferences you happen to have when you die – any more than we have any reason to fulfil preferences you abandoned long ago. But we do have good reason to fulfil preferences you stuck to all your life – and still endorsed when you died. (Another alternative would be to argue that the preferences of a dead person *still exist* in some sense, whereas the past preferences of someone still alive do not exist – perhaps because they have been replaced by later preferences.)

The costs of endorsing posthumous harms may lead us to explore alternative responses to our inconsistent triad. Some preference theorists accept the experience requirement, and offer a different diagnosis of our reluctance to enter the experience machine. The real problem there with the machine is that, once we are in it, we do not know that we are not getting what we want. This does not show that the quality of our experience is irrelevant to well-being – it merely shows that it is not the whole story. The experience machine offers a life where my desires are not fulfilled but I *wrongly believe* that they are. This is undesirable. Posthumous events (however good) can only offer a life where my desires are fulfilled but I *do not know* that they are. This is not satisfactory either. To have a good life, I must have both desires and experiences – I must *know* that my desires have been fulfilled. My desire must be *satisfied*. If we can thus avoid the experience machine and still embrace the experience requirement, then the pressure to reject that requirement dissolves.

How do we count desires?

On the preference theory, the value of a person's life is a function of the extent to which her preferences are satisfied. It may seem that we can determine a person's well-being simply by adding up how many of her desires are satisfied. To compare two lives, we ask which has more desire satisfaction. Unfortunately, things are not so simple. Not all preferences are equally strong, and some lives contain more preferences than others. These factors make it difficult to compare people's overall levels of preference satisfaction, for several reasons.

1. *Quantity versus quality.* One problem is analogous to the threat posed to hedonism by the oyster life. Suppose your physician offers you a new drug treatment that will greatly increase the length of your life, but reduce your intellectual capacities to the point where you can only lie in a hospital bed eating jelly and watching soap operas. (Suppose you like both jelly and soap operas.) If the jelly and soap opera life is long enough, then it will involve more total preference satisfaction than a full human life. So a preference theorist should accept this treatment. Or compare a satisfied turtle with a satisfied human. Who is to say

that the turtle life does not contain more preference satisfaction than the human life? Turtle preferences might be of a more basic kind, but the typical turtle life is so long that it contains many more of them.

2. *Satisfaction versus frustration.* No one in our town has any interest in chocolate. I design an advertising campaign that causes everyone to have an overwhelming desire for chocolate. I then sell chocolate. Exactly half the people buy chocolate, and their desire is satisfied. Unfortunately, not everyone can afford chocolate, so the other half are left with a frustrated desire. I have increased both the level of satisfaction and the level of frustration. Have I made things better or worse?

This question is very significant today, as much of our modern economic activity increases both satisfaction and frustration. There are three possible answers. The first, which many people would endorse, is that I have reduced overall well-being. Creating a desire for chocolate and then satisfying it does no good, but creating a desire I cannot satisfy makes some people worse off. This seemingly plausible position has very radical implications for population policy. If the satisfaction of a desire cannot leave the agent any better off than if she had never had the desire at all, and if the frustration of desires always makes a life worse, then every life is worse than no life at all – as every actual human life includes some frustrated desires. The best possible future would involve the extinction of the human race. As the ancient Greek poet Sophocles put it: "Not to be born is best." (We return to population issues in Chapter 9.)

The second alternative is that I have improved overall well-being, because satisfaction outweighs frustration. Those without chocolate are no worse off than before – there is nothing they had before that they now lack – while those with chocolate are clearly better off. The final alternative is that my actions leave things unchanged, as satisfaction and frustration exactly cancel out. (If I had produced more satisfaction, then I would have improved things.)

It can be difficult to choose between these three alternatives. We may feel this is because chocolate is a trivial example. Perhaps things are clear if we deal with more important desires, such as those in our next two examples.

3. *Undesirable desires.* Sometimes, a new desire clearly seems to make a person's life go much worse, even if it is a very strong

desire that is completely satisfied. I threaten to torture you if you do not give me £10. This creates a very strong desire not to be tortured – much stronger than your desire to keep the money. You give me £10 and I satisfy your desire not to be tortured. I have increased your total level of desire satisfaction – especially if we factor in the strength of the desires involved. Yet it is hard to deny that I make your life worse. If I were charged with obtaining money by the threat of violence, it is unlikely that any judge or jury would accept my defence that I was making your life go better by increasing your level of desire satisfaction!

4. *Desirable desires.* On the other hand, sometimes new desires clearly seem to make a person's life go *better*, even if they are *not all* satisfied. Even though you have no desire for education, I force you to go to school. As a result, your horizons are broadened and you acquire many desires. Many (but not all) of these new desires are then satisfied. My gift of education clearly makes your life better.

The challenge for the preference theorist is to explain the differences between these cases. One tempting move is to appeal to pre-existing desires. In the tale of the threat, you already had a desire not to be tortured. My threat only made you aware of this existing preference. You presumably also had a desire not to be threatened, which I have clearly frustrated. The problem with this response is that most preference theorists regard the conscious intensity of a desire as an indication of its importance. By making you conscious of your desire, I increase the importance of not being tortured. My subsequent decision not to torture you is then a greater benefit. (Your desire not to be tortured is probably stronger than your desire not to be threatened.)

Another solution is to shift from isolated preferences to *global preferences*. Instead of comparing lives by aggregating the preference satisfaction within them, we could take a step back and ask which life is preferable overall. If you prefer the shorter full life to the much longer jelly and soap opera life, then it is better for you. While this move seems intuitively appealing, it is in tension with the foundations of the preference theory. By definition, the jelly and soap opera life involves more preference satisfaction. If you prefer the other life, then you are not choosing between the two lives on the basis of preference satisfaction alone. This suggests that you value something other than preference satisfaction. A theory of well-being that endorses your judgement –

and uses it as the criterion to judge your well-being – has abandoned the preference theory.

The objective list theory

Many utilitarians remain attached to either hedonism or the preference theory. But others conclude that neither theory is satisfactory. Neither pleasure nor preference satisfaction is either necessary or sufficient for well-being. Some pleasures are good, some bad, others are neutral. Some preferences improve your life, while others do not. Consider a child who wants to play in the sand much more than go to school. Overall, many people would agree that we make his life go better if we send him to school. Why is this? One defence of education is that, not only does it help people to satisfy their existing preferences, it also teaches them what to desire. The preference theory has its explanation backwards. It is important to satisfy people's desire *because* what they value is independently worthwhile. The objects are not valuable because they are desired – they are desired because they are valuable. This leads to the *objective list theory*.

I have called the list theory *objective*. This suggests our other two theories are *subjective*. On the most common meaning of the word, this is true. However, in another sense both hedonism and the preference theory are also objective theories. Hedonism says that pleasure is the only valuable thing *for everyone*, no matter what they might happen to think. The preference theory says that, *for everyone*, well-being is the maximizing of preference satisfaction. A purely subjective or *relativistic* theory of well-being, by contrast, would say that well-being *for you* is *whatever you think it is*.

Both hedonism and preference theory could be interpreted as list theories, where pleasure and the absence of pain, or preference satisfaction (or perhaps only preference fulfilment) is the solitary item on our list. Or we could bring hedonism and preference theory together in a list with two items: pleasure and preference satisfaction. Most contemporary list theories include both pleasure and preference satisfaction, either as separate items on the list or as components of other items.

There are two crucial questions to ask about any list. What goes on the list? How do we decide what goes on the list? Although the second question should come first in terms of philosophical method, it is much easier to begin with the first. Here are some items commonly found on the lists offered by contemporary utilitarians.

Components of well-being
1. Basic needs. "What we need to survive, to be healthy, to avoid harm, to function properly." (James Griffin, *Well-being*, 42)
2. Achievement or accomplishment.
3. Understanding or knowledge.
4. Agency, autonomy, freedom.
5. "Friendship" (Shelly Kagan), "deep personal relations" (James Griffin), "mutual love" (Derek Parfit).
6. Religion.
7. Fame or respect.

It is helpful to say a few words about each of these items. The inclusion of basic needs may seem anomalous, as they are not really *components* of a person's well-being, but rather *instrumental necessities* – things every human needs if they are to enjoy any well-being at all. The main reason for including basic needs is not theoretical, but pragmatic, as a focus on basic needs helps us to think about many practical situations, such as the allocation of health care resources. (Are we giving them to those with the greatest basic need?) It also explains the importance many contemporary utilitarians place on helping the victims of famine and disaster.

To count as an independent contribution to your well-being (over and above any pleasure or preference satisfaction), an achievement must involve something that is independently valuable. Finding a cure for cancer or proving a mathematical theorem would count as an *accomplishment*, whereas counting the blades of grass on your lawn would not.

Our third item can include practical knowledge, abstract knowledge, and knowledge of the world and one's place in it. Many philosophers also include *religious* knowledge, which may be either positive (the knowledge that there is a God, accompanied by knowledge of God's purpose for creation) or negative (the knowledge that there is no God).

Our fourth item is perhaps the most important on many lists. It reflects a strong utilitarian tradition established by Mill. Most modern utilitarians attach a very high value to human freedom, especially the ability to make major life choices by deliberating using one's own values. James Griffin goes so far as to call these the "components of human existence" – without them, a life is not genuinely human (Griffin, *Well-being*, 67).

The simplest list theory would calculate the value of your life by adding the values of its components. More subtle approaches posit complex interactions between the items on our list. For instance, pleasure and preference might affect the value of other items, either by enhancing that value or by being a precondition for it. Perhaps other list items only benefit you if you experience them, or if you desire them. (More modestly, other list items might be more valuable if you experience or desire them.) We might combine several preconditions, such as choice and pleasure, or experience and preference. Perhaps knowledge, while always valuable, is much more valuable if it is desired and experienced. Or perhaps knowledge is *only* valuable at all when it is desired and experienced. This does not reduce the value of knowledge to the value of desire, but it does mean that knowledge without desire is not valuable. Or perhaps an accomplishment is only valuable if it is both independently valuable *and* a source of pleasure.

Utilitarians influenced by the liberal tradition of Mill often regard autonomy as an enhancer or precondition of the value of other items. Any list item is only a benefit to you if you have autonomously chosen it. This goes beyond a preference requirement. It is not enough to desire the item. You must have actively and consciously pursued it. Being born a king is no accomplishment, while making yourself king is. This is a common view of the value of religion. Correct religious belief and practice is only valuable if it is freely chosen, not if people are forced to conform.

Friendship could be included under achievement, but it often also appears as a separate item on the list. Recall the person who is betrayed and has no friends at all, but does not know it. We find this life undesirable because it lacks the good of friendship. Placing friendship separately on the list emphasizes the thought that, whatever other achievements it may contain, my life is not truly worthwhile unless it also contains friendship.

Some religiously inclined moral philosophers add religion as a separate list item. They have in mind, not only religious knowledge, but also living your life in accordance with the religious truth, and seeking to establish an appropriate relationship with the divine. Other philosophers, often of a less overtly religious inclination, would incorporate the separate components of religion under other items already on the list, such as knowledge, accomplishment and personal relations. Or we might express the value of religion conditionally: if there is a God, then having an appropriate relationship with God is an essential component of human existence. This would suggest that you cannot know what a good human life would look like unless you know whether or not God exists.

The value of an item, and even whether it is valuable at all, cannot always be evaluated in isolation. It may depend on its place in the context of your life as a whole. We might value *variety* – a list item is more valuable if your life contains few similar items. *Uniqueness* might be especially valuable. A particular accomplishment is much more valuable if you have not done it before. On the other hand, some people value *unity*. An item might be especially valuable in your life precisely because it fits with other things you have done. Or an achievement that would be valuable for someone else might be trivial for you, or even detract from the value of your life, given the high standard set by your other achievements. Thomas Hurka gives the analogy of a sports career. A modest performance at the British Open might detract from the overall value of Tiger Woods' career, even though it would have been the highlight of your golfing life.

All lists are controversial. (Other items often included are: *health, creativity, play, awareness of beauty, living morally*.) How do we justify adding an extra item to our list? Suppose some moral philosopher proposes an item that you do not currently have on your list. How do you decide what to do? For the sake of simplicity, we can imagine an empty list, and ask which items to add. Suppose a new item (x) is proposed for our list. We imagine two otherwise identical lives, where one contains x while the other does not. If the life with x is better than the life without, then x goes on our list. (For example, pleasure.) If the life with x is worse than the life without, then the *absence of x* goes on our list. (For example, pain.) If a life with x seems no better or worse than a life without, then neither x nor the absence of x makes it to our list.

Take a moment to apply this test to each of the items on our list. A good example is fame or respect. This item is not often listed as a separate component of well-being by modern utilitarians, but it was especially popular among the ancient Greeks. The test case for this item is *posthumous fame*. Would it be good for you to be well remembered after your death, even if you do not know about this, and even if it was not something you had ever desired? If you think that posthumous fame is still good, even in these circumstances, then you should include it as a separate item on your list.

This simple method faces a cluster of related objections. Can we construct a single list for everyone? The list theorist faces a dilemma. If their list does apply to everyone, then it may be paternalistic and/or culturally insensitive. Yet, if we have different lists for different folks, then how can the list theorist hope to provide a theory of human well-being, which should unite us rather than divide?

A good place to start is with an objection we first saw in relation to hedonism. Is not the list theory paternalistic, as the person compiling the list must assume that he knows better than we do what is good for us? The list theorist has several replies at this point. The most general is that the list theory need not be paternalistic in its implications for practical morality. Nothing in the notion of a list theory *per se* says that I am better at compiling a list than you. In particular, nothing on the list suggests that I am better placed than you are to know what would count as good *for you*. Indeed, most list theories imply the exact opposite – you are much better placed than anyone else to know what contributes to your well-being. This is especially true if pleasure, preference and autonomy are on the list. Something will only count as good if you endorse it, actively pursue it and take pleasure from it.

The emphasis on autonomy can itself lead to a related objection: that the list theory is too culturally relative to provide a theory of well-being for all human beings. As applied by contemporary philosophers, it produces lists that reflect the values and prejudices of middle-class, affluent, well-educated, Western philosophers (who are also usually middle-aged white males). In particular, it is often said that autonomy is a peculiarly Western value, and that people from other cultures (especially in East Asia) do not value freedom. The standard utilitarian response to this charge is presented especially forcefully by the Nobel Prize winning economist Amartya Sen, who argues at length that, contrary to the claims of undemocratic regimes around the world, people in every culture have always valued the basic freedoms prized by the classical utilitarians – including the freedom to live your own life in accordance with your own values.

Utilitarians will probably agree that many actual lists over-emphasize the priorities of Western philosophers. But they will regard this as a warning to ensure that our list is sensitive to cultural differences, rather than an objection to the list approach *per se*. For instance, including accomplishment on our list does not in itself tell us which accomplishments are valuable. Different cultures might operate with quite different lists of specific accomplishments – as might different individuals within the same culture. Similarly, including freedom in our list does not commit us to any particular theory of what constitutes valuable human freedom. The objective list theory certainly does not prescribe a single ideal life for everyone.

On the other hand, some list items may be almost identical across cultures, even in their specific details. Cultural difference is easy to exaggerate. Would the answers really differ that much across cultures? Would anyone exclude basic needs from their list? A list theorist will go on to conclude that disagreement is no more of a problem here than in other areas of ethics, or in other disciplines such as economics or physics. After all, are non-utilitarian ethical theories any less culture-bound than utilitarianism? If we wish to avoid cultural imperialism, would preference theory or hedonism be any better? Can we live without some implicit theory of what makes life worth living? If we cannot, then perhaps we have to make do with our intuitions, even if they are culture-bound.

A final objection, along similar lines, concerns the possibility that some list items may be positively bad for some people. Is knowledge good for people who do not value it at all, even if it makes them miserable? Suppose you meet someone whose strong religious beliefs give meaning and structure to her life. Unfortunately, her religion is founded on the beliefs that the universe is only a hundred years old and that the earth is flat. You give her a rudimentary education, which completely undermines her religion. Her life loses all meaning, and she cannot function at all. You have given her an item on the list, but it seems you have clearly made her life go worse.

The list theorist has two replies. The first is that, although each item on the list contributes to well-being when considered *in isolation*, this does not mean that giving someone an item on the list is always an improvement in well-being *all things considered*. The good effect of the item itself may be outweighed by its indirect impact. The benefit of knowledge might be outweighed by greater losses, with regard to other items on the list. In the case of the lost faith, knowledge may destroy pleasure, or make it impossible for the person to achieve anything or to form deep personal relations with anyone. Knowledge is then good *in one respect*, but bad *all things considered*.

A second reply is that, while knowledge can be a benefit to someone who does not desire it *in advance*, it must still be valued by the person *at some point*. Recall the child who is reluctantly educated. One clear sign that this constitutes a benefit is that, in later life, the child himself comes to be grateful for the broadening of his desires. He believes his education improved his life. If, in the manner of *The Matrix*, we were to offer him a pill that would enable him to wake up as an uneducated person (with no memory of his education), he would refuse. We might apply the same test to the formerly religious person in our present tale. If she would prefer to return to her previous ignorance, then we might conclude that her new-found knowledge has not benefited her, as she has not endorsed it.

Post hoc endorsement is not infallible. If I brainwash you into rejecting your current desires, then we may regard your subsequent endorsement as more evidence that I have harmed you – not as proof that you have benefited. At this point, proponents of the objective list theory may note that, while it does face problems here, at least it is better placed to solve them than the preference theory. This is because the objective list theory can distance itself more easily for *adaptive preferences* – those that result from social conditioning. The most worrying fact for the preference theory is that, as well as adding preferences, social conditioning can also remove or distort them. If people are deprived of something for long enough, they may lose their desire for it – or never develop the desire in a first place. Slaves express no desire for freedom, nor homeless people for property, nor disenfranchised women for political participation. As the preference theory takes all preferences as given, it thus supports injustice and oppression. If a person has no desire for x, then how can it be wrong to fail to give them x?

Beyond happiness

In its classical formulation, utilitarianism regards happiness as the only value. This raises two questions. Is *all* happiness valuable? Is anything else valuable? We return to the first question in the next section. As with parallel questions regarding both pleasure and preference, the second question is the more controversial. Few contemporary philosophers deny that happiness is important. But is it the only source of value? Even if happiness is the only intrinsic value, many other things are obviously instrumentally valuable. So our real question is whether anything else is intrinsically valuable. Just as the objective list theory points to values beyond pleasure and preference, it also raises the possibility of values beyond happiness. If the appreciation of beauty is intrinsically valuable, then perhaps beauty itself is valuable even if there is no one to appreciate it. In the early twentieth century, G. E. Moore used the following thought experiment against Sidgwick's broadly hedonist account of well-being.

> **Two empty worlds**
> Imagine two possible universes. Neither contains any human beings or other sentient creatures. One universe is extremely beautiful, the other very ugly. Which is better?

Moore argues that the first universe is much better. Suppose you are the last human. All other animals are extinct. You can arrange for a huge bomb to detonate at your death, leaving the world ugly. A utilitarian such as Sidgwick would find nothing wrong with this. Yet surely it is very wrong indeed.

Some utilitarians simply reject Moore's intuition. Others try to explain it away. Natural beauty is instrumentally valuable because it gives people pleasure. Many naturally beautiful things are also instrumentally useful in other ways. So we have a strong aversion to the gratuitous destruction of natural beauty. This aversion carries over to Moore's artificial case, even though the utilitarian rationale no longer applies.

The objective list theory fits nicely with Moore's intuition. Indeed, it is hard to see how such a theory could survive without *some* independent values. How can we say that an achievement contributes to well-being because of its independent value if it has no independent value?

The objective list theory thus produces an uneasy form of utilitarianism. If we believe that all values must be ultimately reducible to happiness, then the fact that it points beyond the consciousness of sentient beings is a strike against the objective list theory. On the other hand, if we want to admit both the value of happiness and the existence of values independent of humanity, then the objective list theory provides a plausible bridge between the two.

Non-human animals

We finish our discussion of well-being by applying our three theories to non-human animals. If we are sure of our theory of well-being for humans, then we can extend it to non-human animals to discover how we should treat them. On the other hand, if we are more sure of our beliefs about the relationship between humans and non-humans, we can use those beliefs to test our theories of well-being. For instance, if you are sure that animals and humans are not on a par, then you will reject any theory of well-being that cannot distinguish them.

Suppose you are a hedonist. Human lives matter because they contain pleasure and pain. Many non-human animals can enjoy pleasure and suffer pain. If human lives matter, then so should the lives of these animals. Instead of maximizing human happiness, utilitarians should maximize happiness *per se*. Animals should count just as much as humans.

The practical consequences of the moral equivalence of humans and non-humans are both obvious and radical. Many human practices cause suffering to animals that is vastly out of proportion to any resulting human pleasure. Humans need to eat and to enjoy themselves. But we could eat plants and play harmless games rather than killing animals for food and sport. It is no coincidence that one of the most influential figures in the animal liberation movement has been a utilitarian philosopher – Peter Singer.

Most utilitarians agree that the welfare of animals must count for something. However, not everyone places animals on a par with humans. A hedonist might argue that only humans can experience the higher pleasures. If a philosophy life is better than a pig life, and only humans can enjoy the philosophy life, then utilitarians should pay more attention to humans. Preference theorists can make a similar move. Although non-human animals have desires, perhaps human desires are more sophisticated and complex, and thus count for more. (This is not to deny that some preference theorists do reach radical conclusions regarding animal rights. Singer himself, for instance, adopts a preference-based account of well-being on which animal suffering is very bad because animals have a strong aversion to pain.) The objective list theory can go even further, as many items on our list may be completely unavailable to non-human animals. (While pigs can prefer mud to concrete, they probably cannot autonomously pursue a life devoted to pushing back the boundaries of mathematical knowledge.)

If animal happiness differs from human happiness, then as well as counting animals less than humans, we may also be allowed to do some things to animals that we must not do to humans. To test our intuitions, consider two cases.

The replicas

I have developed a machine that can painlessly kill a creature, and then replace it with an almost exact replica. The only difference is that the replica is slightly happier than the original creature. I use the machine on Bob.

> **The friendly farmer**
> Bob lives in a field on my farm. Bob has a very pleasant life and is unaware of his fate. One day, I painlessly and instantaneously kill Bob. His body is made into burgers.

In both cases, most people think I have behaved very badly if Bob is a human being. (We discuss the replicas tale further in Chapter 5, where we shall see that many of its opponents argue that utilitarianism sanctions this sort of treatment even in the case of humans.) But do you feel the same if I tell you that Bob is a cow? What about a cockroach or a dog or a pig or a monkey or a dolphin or a Klingon? If your intuitions do differ, are you irrationally favouring your own species, or can your responses be given a good utilitarian justification?

Key points

- The three main theories of well-being are hedonism (happiness is pleasure), preference theory (happiness is getting what you want), and objective list theory (happiness is getting things that are independently valuable).
- The key test for hedonism is Nozick's experience machine. If you would not enter the machine, then you are not a hedonist.
- The key tests for preference theory are non-I desires, irrational desires, posthumous desires and the aggregation of desires.
- The key tests for the objective list theory are cultural relativism, paternalism, and whether list items are good for someone who does not want them.
- Another key test for any theory of well-being is whether it explains the value of animal well-being.

five

Injustice and demands

Fourteen tales of injustice and unreasonable demand

Intuitive objections to utilitarianism come in two main types. Utilitarianism is accused of requiring you to do things to other people that you ought not to, and of forbidding you from doing things for yourself that you should be allowed to do. We might call these *injustice objections* and *demandingness objections* respectively. Both objections are best introduced using simple stories, some already familiar from earlier chapters. Stories 1–9 relate to injustice objections; 10–12 are demandingness objections; while in our final two tales utilitarianism forces you both to sacrifice yourself and to behave unjustly to others.

1. *The sheriff.* You are the sheriff in an isolated wild-west town. A murder has been committed. Most people believe that Bob is guilty, but you know he is innocent. Unless you hang Bob now, there will be a riot in town and several people will die. Utilitarianism says you must hang Bob, because the loss of his life is outweighed by the value of preventing the riot.

2. *The transplant.* You are a doctor at a hospital. You have five patients who will each die without an immediate transplant. One patient needs a new heart, two need a new lung, and two need a new kidney. Mary comes into a hospital for a routine checkup. By a remarkable coincidence, Mary is a suitable donor for all five patients. Utilitarianism says you should arrange for Mary to

die unexpectedly on the operating table, as the loss of her life is outweighed by the lives of the five patients.

3. *The torturer.* You are a law enforcement officer interrogating a known terrorist who has admitted to planting a bomb in a crowded area of the city. He will not tell you where it is. The only way to get the terrorist to confess is to torture his innocent child. Utilitarianism says you should torture the child, as her suffering is outweighed by the many lives you will save if you disarm the bomb.

4. *The trolley.* You are standing on a bridge with your friend Albert when you see a railway trolley carrying ten people rushing out of control toward a washed-out bridge. Unless you stop the trolley, it will plunge over a steep cliff and ten people will die. The only way to stop the trolley is to push Albert in front of it. His collision with the trolley will kill Albert, but it will make the trolley stop before the cliff. Utilitarianism says you should push Albert, as his life is outweighed by the lives of the ten people in the trolley.

5. *The Archbishop and the chambermaid.* You are trapped in a burning building with two other people. One is an Archbishop who is "a great benefactor of mankind" and the other is a chambermaid who happens to be your mother. You only have time to save one person from the fire. Utilitarianism says you should save the Archbishop, as he contributes more to human happiness than the chambermaid. (This old example is from William Godwin, who endorsed the conclusion, as we saw in Chapter 2. If you doubt that Archbishops are more useful than chambermaids, you should rewrite the story – replacing the Archbishop with someone genuinely useful.)

6. *The game.* The soccer World Cup final is being broadcast live around the world to an audience of several billion people. You are in charge of the power transmitter nearest the stadium. Hapless Harry has become trapped in power lines at the transmitter. The only way to save Harry is to shut the transmitter down for fifteen minutes. This would deprive several billion people of the pleasure of watching the final 15 minutes of the World Cup final. Utilitarianism says you should not rescue Harry, as his agonizing death is outweighed by all those billions of units of pleasure.

7. *The replicas.* You have developed a machine that can painlessly kill a person, and then replace them with an almost exact replica. The only difference is that the replica is slightly happier than the

original person. Utilitarianism says you should use this machine on everyone you meet, as this increases human happiness.

8. *Christians and lions.* You are the ancient Roman official responsible for entertainment at the Colosseum. There is a full house. The crowd is uninterested in chariot races or athletics, or even gladiatorial contests. What would give them most pleasure is to see a small group of Christians eaten alive by hungry lions. Utilitarianism says you should feed the Christians to the lions, as their suffering is outweighed by the pleasure of many thousands of spectators.

9. *Efficient slavery.* You are in charge of economic policy in a society whose economy is built on slavery. (Imagine ancient Greece, or England in the eighteenth century, or the Southern USA in the nineteenth century.) You must decide whether to abolish slavery. Without the free labour provided by slaves, your manufacturers and exporters would be unable to compete. Utilitarianism says you should retain the institution of slavery, as the suffering of slaves is outweighed by the benefits to producers and consumers.

10. *The envelope.* On your desk is an envelope addressed to a reputable charity seeking donations to save the lives of victims of a famine or other natural disaster. Utilitarianism says you should give *all* your money to this charity, as each dollar will produce more happiness in their hands than you could possibly produce by spending it in any other way.

11. *The charitable life.* You see an advertisement on television from a charitable organization calling for volunteers to spend the next thirty years working with destitute people in a very poor country. Utilitarianism says you should drop whatever else you might be doing and volunteer, as this would produce more happiness than anything else you could do with your life.

12. *The reluctant banker.* You must decide whether to become a teacher or a merchant banker. Although you find it very unfulfilling, you have a natural aptitude for banking. You calculate that, if you become a banker and donate all your earnings to charity, this will produce more happiness for others than if you do anything else with your life. Your misery is outweighed by the happiness of the recipients of charity. Utilitarianism says you should become a banker.

13. *The broken promise.* You and your friend Betty are competing in the doubles sculls competition in the Olympics. You have both

trained for this event many hours a day every day for several years, and made huge sacrifices to get to the final. On the day of the final, you see the advertisement from the charitable organization in Tale 11. They need volunteers immediately. You calculate that, even if you win the gold medal, this will not produce as much happiness as you can produce by leaving immediately for the afflicted area. Utilitarianism says you must leave, abandoning Betty and rendering all her work and sacrifice pointless.

14. *The small country dilemma.* You and Betty have reached the final at the Olympics. You are representing New Zealand, a small country. In final stages of the race you and Betty are leading, followed by the team from India, a very populous country. Neither New Zealand nor India win many gold medals. You realize that the victors will bring happiness to everyone in their country. Utilitarianism says you should give up, allowing the team from India to win, as this will give happiness to many more people.

In each tale, the objection is that utilitarianism gives the wrong answer. It either allows you to do something monstrous or prevents you from doing something perfectly acceptable. (It may be useful to pause at this point to examine whether, in each tale, utilitarianism really does say what its opponents allege it says, and then (if it does) whether that implication really is so objectionable.) Although they seem quite different, all fourteen objections have a common structure. Utilitarians are only interested in the total amount of happiness. They are not at all interested in *how* happiness is produced, or in *whose* happiness is at stake. The general objection is that, as moral agents, we *should* care about these two things. Sometimes it does matter how happiness is produced or whose happiness is involved. In the sheriff, transplant, torturer and trolley cases, you should not sacrifice one person's happiness simply to maximize total happiness. Overall happiness is trumped by moral prohibitions on certain sorts of actions: murdering innocent people, murdering your own patients, torturing an innocent child, or pushing someone in front of the trolley.

The wrongness of the action is increased in each case by the fact that you stand in a special relationship to the person you sacrifice. You have a particular obligation not to harm them in this way. Sheriffs, of all people, should not hang the innocent. Murder is bad enough, but doctors especially owe a duty of care to their patients. It would be bad enough to push a stranger in front of the trolley, but it is even worse if Albert is your friend.

In the tales of unreasonable demand, utilitarianism fails because it does not allow you to give special weight to your own interests and projects, and to those of people who are close to you. You should be allowed to save your mother from the fire, or to favour yourself. It is unreasonable to expect anyone to be perfectly impartial. Just as you are not allowed to sacrifice others, you cannot be required to sacrifice yourself.

To highlight the connections between the two types of objection, we could retell all the injustice tales in the first person, thereby generating new tales of unreasonable demand. Suppose Bob, who knows he is innocent, has escaped from custody. He knows there will be a riot unless he allows himself to be hanged. Does utilitarianism require that he turn himself in? Suppose you discover that *you* are a suitable match for each of your five dying patients. Does utilitarianism require you to donate your own heart, lungs and kidneys, even at the cost of your life? Suppose you *are* the terrorist's child. Does utilitarianism oblige you to volunteer to be tortured? Suppose you are alone by the railway track as the trolley hurtles towards you. Does utilitarianism require you to throw yourself in front of the trolley to save ten lives? In all these cases, while we might *admire* someone who made this sacrifice, few of us regard it as obligatory.

Explaining the inadequacy of utilitarianism

Opponents of utilitarianism offer several related explanations for its failure. The first is that utilitarianism ignores the crucial moral distinction between *doing* and *allowing*; especially the distinction between *killing* someone and *allowing them to die*. As utilitarians are only interested in the consequences, they cannot make these distinctions. A utilitarian sheriff does not see a choice between killing an innocent person and allowing a riot. They see only the results: one person dies or several people die. A utilitarian cannot see that the sheriff is *responsible* for Bob's death but not for the riot. On the other hand, because they think failing to donate to save someone's life is just as bad as killing them, utilitarians must constantly donate.

> The striking feature of the utilitarian view of justice is that it does not matter, except indirectly, how this sum of satisfactions is distributed among individuals any more than it matters, except indirectly, how one man distributes his

satisfactions over time. The correct distribution in either case is that which yields the maximum fulfillment. . . . Utilitarianism does not take seriously the distinction between persons.

(Rawls, *A Theory of Justice*, 26–7)

Rawls' complaint provides both a striking *example* of the unjust and unreasonable demands of utilitarianism and an *explanation* of those demands. Utilitarians ignore the fact that each life is separate. So they cannot see why it is wrong to sacrifice one person for others, or why it is unreasonable to expect each agent to sacrifice herself for others. Lacking an adequate theory of human nature, utilitarianism cannot even see why its results are unjust and its demands unreasonable. Utilitarianism places unreasonable demands on moral agents simply because it does not understand what moral agents are like.

Any ethic which requires people to be agents . . . must on pain of absurdity permit agent-related partialism.

(Cottingham, "Partiality, Favouritism and Morality", 365)

Some philosophers object that, because it ignores the separateness of persons, utilitarianism fails to count as a moral theory at all. Adequate moral theories must proceed from a picture of human agency that is inconsistent with utilitarianism. If utilitarianism forbids any partiality, then it cannot be taken seriously as a moral theory.

How can a man, as a utilitarian agent, come to regard as one satisfaction among others, and a dispensable one, a project or attitude round which he has built his life?

(Bernard Williams, in Smart & Williams, *Utilitarianism: For and Against*, 116)

Williams' complaint is often called the "integrity objection". The term "integrity" can mislead. This does not refer to a separable valuable component of a good life, or to moral uprightness. Rather, the integrity of a life is its wholeness, unity or shape. Williams speaks of the integrity of a human life in the same way that we might speak of the integrity of a work of art. By requiring every agent to give her own welfare no more weight than the welfare of others, utilitarianism undermines the *integrity* of the agent's life. The utilitarian agent must view every life from the outside, seeing only its contribution to the overall value of the universe. So we must each view our own life only from this impersonal perspective. But no agent who views her own life this way can flourish.

The integrity and separateness objections are clearly related. Part of what it is to see one's life as an integrated whole is precisely to see it as distinct from the lives of others. The two notions are two sides of the same coin. If utilitarianism ignores one, it is not surprising that it overlooks the other. Peter Railton expresses a similar objection in terms of *alienation* – "a kind of estrangement resulting in some sort of loss" (Railton, "Alienation, Utilitarianism and Morality", 93). By requiring us always to adopt the impersonal perspective, utilitarianism alienates us from our own lives. No utilitarian agent can live a meaningful life, as they cannot identify with their own projects.

The violation of integrity and the risk of alienation are also striking examples of the unreasonable demands of utilitarianism. Naive utilitarians might argue that their theory only requires you to give up money, which is not a vital component of human flourishing. They might even suggest that you would be better off without the distractions of consumer society. Opponents will reply that utilitarianism not only requires you to sacrifice resources that you could have devoted to your own projects; it also requires you to be prepared to abandon those projects immediately should they cease to be your most effective way of maximizing the impersonal good. Yet, if you are constantly prepared to abandon your projects whenever the utilitarian calculus demands, you cannot really commit to those projects at all.

This is a very significant point. The force of any demandingness objection is a function, not only of the number of demands a given theory makes, but also of the moral significance of each demand to the individual agent. Some components or aspects of well-being may be more significant than others. For instance, we may judge the demand that I give up my freedom more harshly than the demand that I relinquish most of my worldly possessions, even though the latter leaves me worse off than the former.

Extremism

Each of our objections has a simple structure. Utilitarianism is unacceptable because (a) it says *x* and (b) no acceptable moral theory would say *x*. (Where *x* is some claim like "Sheriffs should murder to prevent riots", "Everyone should give all their money to charity", and so on.) Utilitarians have three possible replies. They can defend *x* (pages

100–3), deny that utilitarianism says *x* (pages 104–12), or agree that utilitarianism gets the wrong result in this particular case but deny that a single counterexample is sufficient to rule out an otherwise promising moral theory (pages 103–4).

We begin with the first option. The simplest, and most extreme, utilitarian response to all our objections is to reject the use of *particular* intuitions to test a moral theory. However counter-intuitive or demanding morality turns out to be, we cannot reject its demands simply because we find them unpalatable. If we define the notion of a "reasonable demand" in utilitarian terms, then a demand is unreasonable only if the sacrifice involved (for the agent or others) is greater than the increase in total welfare. By definition, the demands of utilitarianism are not unreasonable. No sheriff is required to hang an innocent person if no good will come of it, and no affluent person is required to throw her happiness away unless she can do more good for others.

Following Shelly Kagan, let us call a utilitarian who endorses these extreme demands, an *extremist*. Extremists usually begin with an (allegedly) uncontroversial moral principle, such as one of those discussed in Chapter 3: the reason to promote the good, the principle of harm prevention, or the principle of aid to innocents. The extremist then rejects all departures from their utilitarian starting point. So the starting point must now represent the whole of morality, however counter-intuitive or demanding that may seem.

> The way people do in fact judge has nothing to do with the validity of my conclusion.
>
> (Singer, "Famine, Affluence and Morality", 236)

Some extremists simply reject particular moral intuitions altogether. In *The Limits of Morality*, Kagan argues that intuitions need a *rationale*. Kagan presents common-sense morality as a moderate position, situated between extremism (utilitarianism) and minimalism (egoism). Common-sense morality agrees that we are sometimes required to sacrifice our own interests for the greater good. So it must explain why we are not always required to promote the good. Common-sense morality must include *options*, permitting agents to pursue their own projects at the expense of the overall good. Kagan then argues that, if common-sense morality includes options, then it must also include *constraints* prohibiting certain actions, such as killing or lying. Kagan considers two possible rationales for constraints: the distinction between doing and allowing, and the distinction between intending and foreseeing. He argues that the former can only be defended if the latter is presupposed. He then rejects the latter. Far from being self-evident, the intuition that morality should not be very demanding is based on a very unstable foundation.

The rejection of intuitions is often backed up by a deflationary explanation of their origins. If our moral intuitions are the products of evolution, culture or self-interest, then extremists argue that they are unreliable. In particular, many extremists argue that the anti-utilitarian intuition that morality must not be too demanding merely serves our own interests, and does not reflect a balanced view of the world. Singer argues that, if people (a) were better informed; (b) reasoned more clearly; and (c) were better able to imagine what life is like for those who are destitute, then they would no longer regard the demands of utilitarianism as unreasonable. (Singer also employs an analogous strategy to show that conventional morality unjustly ignores the interests of non-human animals.) Singer's consciousness raising is not just a practical strategy. It also has a theoretical dimension. Our particular intuitions must be brought into reflective equilibrium with general intuitions about when particular intuitions are (and are not) reliable. Some intuitions do not survive a careful examination of where they come from.

A similar, though more complex, process of reflection might undermine the intuition that utilitarianism is unjust. This intuition assumes that obligations to particular individuals can outweigh the general good. A utilitarian might object that, while it seems reasonable to us, this general idea benefits those who are better-off. Even if special obligations apply to everyone, their overall impact clearly benefits the affluent, whose special obligations to one another ensure that their own disproportionate share of resources is devoted even more disproportionately to themselves. Against a background of unequal resource distribution, the recognition of special obligations serves to exacerbate inequality. Thomas Nagel makes this point in a vivid way. Imagine that rich people in the developed world and poor people in the developing world have come together to find moral principles to govern their interactions. Nagel argues that, given the present state of the world, the poor would reasonably reject any set of principles allowing the rich to protect their existing property rights and mutual support obligations, thereby avoiding significant donations to famine relief.

Non-utilitarians are seldom convinced by extremism. Extremists set a very high standard of proof for departures from their utilitarian starting point. Could that starting point itself meet such a standard?

The intuitions behind the objection to utilitarianism are at least as strong as those behind the extremist's utilitarian starting point.

> To most people, it is about as obvious that there is a moral difference between our relations to a child drowning in front of us and a child starving in another country as it is that failing to save a drowning child is wrong.
>
> (Cullity, "International Aid and the Scope of Kindness", 5)

Many moderate moral theorists also reject Kagan's claim that everyone accepts the utilitarian's reason to promote the good. They replace a general reason to promote the good with a number of more specific principles deriving reasons for action from features of possible outcomes. Few (if any) moral theorists deny that we often have reason to promote particular goods in particular situations. However, some *do* reject a general reason to promote the good, often because they reject the utilitarian idea that goodness is a general property of possible states of affairs, as opposed to a particular property of individual things. I can make this person's life go better, but I cannot make "things overall" go better. (Of course, even among those who do accept the idea of a general reason to promote the good, many will object to the details of any specific utilitarian account of what goodness is – as we shall see on pages 107–12.) If some plausible moderate theories reject the extremist's starting point, then the case for extremism is only as strong as the case for that starting point itself.

A crucial issue here is the relationship between particular cases and general principles. Like many moral philosophers, extremists often begin with a moral judgement relating to a simple story, and then produce a general principle – of which the initial judgement is said to be a particular instance. Unfortunately, in ethics as in science, the data underdetermine the theory. Even if we agree with the extremists' particular judgement, we may disagree with their general principle. Extremists often use a very controversial *utilitarian* account of ethical generalization. For instance, Singer's example of the drowning child might generate a very limited duty to save people in dire need in your immediate vicinity, rather than a general duty to avoid harm. Could extremists sell their reason to promote the good to someone who was as sceptical about utilitarianism as the extremist is about departures from utilitarianism? The recent history of moral philosophy suggests not.

A second style of argument for extremism turns less on moral intuitions and more on considerations drawn from metaphysics. Recall Rawls' accusation that utilitarians ignore the separateness of persons.

One obvious reply is that the separateness of persons *should* be ignored, because it is not metaphysically significant. Following the contemporary Oxford philosopher Derek Parfit, some utilitarians defend a *reductionist* account of personal identity. People are made up of experiences standing in various relations to one another. There is nothing to a person beyond those experiences. The boundaries between one life and another are not as morally significant as we think. If the boundary between people is not metaphysically significant, then there is no reason why I should be more concerned for my own future experiences than for anyone else's. If I value future experiences at all, I should value them all equally. This leads us to utilitarianism.

David Brink attacks Rawls from the opposite direction. Parfit suggests we see people as wholes made up of parts (experiences). Brink views each person as themselves a part of a greater whole. The interests of different agents are interrelated, not separate and conflicting. Brink identifies this view with both ancient Greek philosophers and nineteenth-century British Idealists, especially Sidgwick's friend T. H. Green. Indeed, Brink notes that "Green goes so far as to claim that when each is engaged in proper self-realisation, there can be no conflict or competition of interests" (Brink, "Self-love and Altruism", 135). Once again, the separateness of persons is not fundamental.

These metaphysical arguments are controversial. Non-utilitarians may simply reject Parfit's reductionism or Green's Hegelian metaphysics. Or they might deny that these metaphysical claims support utilitarianism. (Green himself actually used Hegelian metaphysics to attack Mill's particular form of utilitarianism.) Or non-utilitarians might argue that moral philosophy should be independent of metaphysics. For instance, the contemporary Kantian philosopher Christine Korsgaard suggests that Parfit's metaphysical arguments only establish, at best, that we can do metaphysics without a separate concept of "person". But we cannot do moral philosophy without persons, because moral philosophers must think of themselves (and others) as agents continuing through time – making choices and carrying out plans.

Utilitarianism is not alone

Another way to defend utilitarianism is to argue that, although it produces extreme results, so do all its competitors. Counter-intuitive results are inevitable in our world. We naturally think both that there are limits to the demands of morality and that those demands depend on the state of the world. In a world with vast unmet need, these two appealing ideals inevitably conflict. Even the ordinary non-utilitarian notion of a duty of benevolence can threaten to be extremely demanding, if it requires me to save someone's life *whenever* I can do so at negligible cost to myself. (After a while, a whole stream of negligible costs has a major impact on my life.)

Utilitarians also present tales where any non-utilitarian view gives counter-intuitive results. Recall the following tale from Chapter 3.

The rocks

Six innocent swimmers have become trapped on two rocks by the incoming tide. Five of the swimmers are on one rock, while the last swimmer is on the second rock. Each swimmer will drown unless they are rescued. You are the sole lifeguard on duty. You have time to get to one rock in your patrol-boat and save everyone on it. Because of the distance between the rocks, and the speed of the tide, you cannot get to both rocks in time. What should you do?

Clearly you should go to the first rock – saving five lives rather than one. Utilitarianism offers a simple explanation – saving five produces more happiness. Some non-utilitarians focus instead on your obligations to particular individuals. Yet you seem to have exactly the same obligation to the person trapped on his own as to the other five. So you have no reason to save the five.

Utilitarianism thus highlights problems faced by all moral theorists. Similar tensions exist elsewhere. Are torture and murder really off-limits no matter what? How should the government balance the competing needs of medical technology, road safety and crime prevention? If utilitarianism is not the right way to answer these questions, then what is?

We return to non-utilitarian approaches to morality in Chapter 7. In the meantime, we examine attempts to revise utilitarianism to make it more intuitively appealing. The rest of this chapter explores revised utilitarian accounts of value, while Chapters 6 and 7 examine alternative accounts of the relationship between value and right action. We begin with a last attempt to avoid revision.

Strategies of denial

Another common utilitarian strategy is to deny that the theory produces such counter-intuitive results. Despite first appearances, utilitarianism does not require sheriffs to murder the innocent, or oblige you to donate everything to charity. Utilitarians pursue one of two broad strategies. They either defend traditional utilitarianism or develop a revised utilitarianism with more intuitive implications. This section examines the first option. We focus on two factors cited by defenders of traditional utilitarianism: our ignorance of consequences and our ignorance of the needs of distant strangers.

Due to the complexity of the causal processes involved, we cannot ever be certain what results our actions will have in the long term, or in some far distant place. Injustice is not a good strategy in these circumstances. The sheriff knows that hanging Bob has a definite negative impact on welfare (Bob dies). The alleged positive result is much less certain. The sheriff cannot know either that the riot definitely *will* happen if Bob is not hanged, or that it definitely *will not* happen if he is. Hanging Bob might also produce additional negative consequences. If Bob is later proved innocent, then public confidence in law enforcement is undermined, the sheriff loses his job and his family starve. Even if no one ever finds out what he has done, the sheriff himself may suffer psychological trauma or guilt for years afterwards, perhaps leading to a breakdown or serious lapse of judgement in the future. So a utilitarian sheriff should play it safe and not hang Bob.

Similar arguments apply to our other tales. The law enforcement officer does not know either that the terrorist will not confess without the torture, or that he will confess with it. You do not know that the trolley will not stop on its own, and you cannot be sure that Albert will stop it. If you push Albert onto the tracks, you might simply be adding extra horror to the dying moments of the ten people in the trolley. Colosseum crowds are notoriously fickle – perhaps the last thing they really want is yet another bout of lions versus Christians. The economics of slavery are so uncertain – perhaps the need to boost productivity to pay market wages to former slaves will fuel an economic boom. New technology is unreliable – how do I know the replicas will be happy? There is also an analogous reply to the demandingness objections. If I spend my money on myself or my friends, then I can be fairly sure my actions will have a positive impact on human welfare. I cannot be nearly as confident that my donation to a charity operating in a distant country will do good. As a utilitarian, I should focus on maximizing happiness closer to home.

Its opponents argue that utilitarianism's aversion to torture is not sufficiently robust. Even if utilitarianism happens to give the right results in our particular tales (or in real life), this is not enough. An adequate moral theory should give the right answers *for the right reasons*. Its judgements should be reliable and robust. Even if it is very unlikely that a sheriff is certain that killing an innocent person would prevent a riot, this situation is not impossible. And utilitarianism must say that, if you *are* certain it would do more good, then you *must* kill the innocent person. This is enough, according to its opponents, to discredit utilitarianism.

Furthermore, many are suspicious whether utilitarianism really can give the right answers, even in our original tales. It is not true that utilitarians should *always* focus on immediate or more certain consequences. Once the sheriff weighs up the values and probabilities involved, he may well conclude that, although hanging Bob is not *certain* to produce good results, it does have a higher *expected value*. (The expected value of an action is the sum of the value of each possible outcome multiplied by its probability. For further discussion, see Chapter 8.) It seems very unlikely that no sheriff has ever been in *this* position.

In relation to the demandingness objections, the utilitarian argument from ignorance might have been much more credible in the nineteenth century than today, as the expected value of trying to send money to aid the distant poor was then very low. (On the other hand, nineteenth-century Britain offered affluent people many opportunities to help extremely poor people much closer to home – so the overall demands of utilitarianism would still have been very severe.) Nowadays, however, extremists such as Singer argue that we can place our money in the hands of much more reliable aid agencies, who can generally provide comparatively accurate estimates of the expected value of a given donation.

At this point, utilitarians might be tempted by a different argument, based on our *knowledge* of probabilities rather than our ignorance – the *Malthusian Argument*, named for the nineteenth-century British economist Robert Malthus. This very common argument agrees that we are able to improve and safeguard the lives of those who are currently starving. It then draws the conclusion that this would be an undesirable result. If we aid starving people, then more of them will live to maturity. As the birth rate in poor countries is often very high, this will lead to an unsustainable population explosion. Unpleasant as it may seem, a high rate of infant mortality is necessary in the long term.

The simplest response to this argument is that all the empirical evidence to date suggests that Malthus was completely wrong. Increases in the standard of living tend to be followed by *decreases* in the birth rate, with the overall result that population growth is reduced. Furthermore, even where population has expanded rapidly, both life expectancy and average material standard of living have tended to rise rather than fall. The lesson for utilitarians is that they should be careful how they spend their aid, not that they can justify giving nothing.

Finally, a defender of utilitarianism might appeal to our ignorance about the values of possible outcomes. We know what is good for ourselves and our friends, whereas we do not know what will be good for distant strangers. Even if we knew everything about the practical situation of the strangers, we could not know what would count as a benefit to them, as their notion of a worthwhile human life might be radically different from our own. So utilitarianism is not very demanding, as it will not require you to come to the assistance of those in distant lands.

Most opponents of utilitarianism (together with most utilitarians) find this argument unconvincing. While we may not know the more sophisticated interests or values of distant strangers, we surely do know that they need clean water, freedom from curable diseases, adequate food and shelter, and some element of peace and stability. To deny that needs as basic as these are cross-cultural is to embrace a cultural relativism of the most absurd sort. Also, while we may not know precisely what distant strangers need, we can always donate our money to charitable organizations who do know. To argue that our own ignorance prevents us from effectively rendering assistance is like saying it is pointless for medically ignorant citizens to fund hospitals.

Rethinking value

Some of the objections raised in this chapter rest on a particular account of how utilitarians calculate human happiness. Utilitarians can avoid those objections by rejecting that picture. There are three general strategies available: to rethink what welfare is; to question whether welfare is the only thing that really matters to utilitarians; and to rethink how welfare is aggregated.

Rethinking welfare

Utilitarians might deny that great suffering for a single person can be outweighed by a tiny pleasure for each of a sufficient number of people. They have two options: to deny that the morally dubious option in tales such as the game, Christians and lions, or efficient slavery really does maximize total human welfare; or to deny that utilitarians are committed to maximize total well-being *no matter what*. We begin with the first option. One reason why we find these tales so troubling is that we do not believe that small pleasures are the sort of thing that can morally outweigh great suffering, an agonizing death, or the degradation of living as a slave. Some components of human well-being are not just more important than others, but *lexically* more important.

Lexicality is a key concept in contemporary moral philosophy. Think of the way words are ordered in a dictionary. Although each letter in a word plays a role in determining its place in the dictionary, the first letter trumps the others. "Azure" comes before "Baal". The first letter is *lexically more important* than the second.

Many contemporary philosophers think values are lexically ordered. Although small pleasures are valuable, their value is not measured on the same scale as higher values, such as enjoying a life free from agony, premature death or slavery. No amount of small pleasure compensates for the loss of these higher values. Suppose you enjoy eating chocolate. Is there any amount of chocolate-eating pleasure that would tempt you to accept an agonizing death or to agree to be a slave? If not, then a free life without agony is lexically more valuable to you than the pleasure of eating chocolate. If you are a utilitarian, then no amount of chocolate-eating pleasure for some people could justify the agonizing death of someone else.

In some of our tales, there are further reasons for utilitarians to resist the proposed course of action. For instance, utilitarians who are not hedonists have a reply to the replicas tale. Replacing a person with a slightly happier replica may increase total *pleasure*, but it does not maximize *human well-being*. The basic unit of human well-being is a human life. Suppose you die at forty, having spent your life preparing to prove a great mathematical theorem. You are then replaced by a slightly happier replica, who goes on to prove the theorem. For a hedonist, this is just as good as if you had proved the theorem yourself. But a preference theorist or an objective list theorist will think otherwise. *No one* enjoys the achievement of preparing-for-the-proof-and-then-proving-it. You die with your project uncompleted, while your replica's achievement is hollow – he or she has not done anything to deserve it. (You do have the achievement of laying-the-necessary-groundwork-for-the-proof, but that is not the same.)

Similar considerations apply to other key components of welfare. Suppose even his closest friends and family cannot tell Bobby and his replica apart. They all think he came home from work today slightly happier than usual. (The replica is also fooled – he thinks he is Bobby.) When he was replaced, Bobby had been married to Mary for twenty years. His replica lives another twenty years. Mary thinks she has enjoyed a forty-year marriage with Bobby. But she has actually enjoyed a twenty-year marriage with Bobby, followed by twenty (slightly happier) years with a complete stranger. A hedonist cannot tell the difference. But either a preference theorist or an objective list theorist can conclude that things go worse for Mary (and for Bobby/replica), than if he had not been replaced.

Finally, as we saw in Chapter 4, some utilitarians deny that sadistic pleasures contribute to a person's well-being. If I gain enjoyment from watching someone else suffer, then this does not make my life go better. If the spectacle in the Colosseum would not contribute to human happiness at all, then you have no obligation to provide that spectacle. Of course, this solution will not work in other situations, such as the tale of the game, where the spectator's pleasure is not sadistic. In the game, the pleasure involved is the enjoyment of a game of football. While Hapless Harry's torment is necessary for the viewers to enjoy this pleasure, this is accidental. They do not know Harry is suffering, and they do not take pleasure in his suffering. (Indeed, if they did know he was suffering, that might ruin their enjoyment of the game.) In Christians and lions, the link between suffering and pleasure is much more direct. What gives the spectators pleasure is the very fact that the Christians are being eaten alive. It seems especially repugnant to count this sort of sadistic pleasure as a reason for providing the spectacle.

Utilitarianism and welfare

Some accounts of well-being (especially hedonism) do believe that sadistic pleasure improves the person's life – at least if other things are equal. If we want our utilitarian theory to be consistent with these accounts of well-being, then we might admit that a person's sadistic pleasures do contribute to their happiness. We could then deny that utilitarians should take such pleasures into account. Perhaps only morally acceptable pleasures or preferences, those that are not directly sadistic, should count. We might then go further, and argue that utilitarians should only respond to basic needs, and ignore more esoteric preferences. As T. M. Scanlon suggests, I might feel obliged to provide you with food but not to help you build a temple to your god – even though I know you would rather complete the temple than stay alive.

A more extreme move in the same direction is *negative utilitarianism*. Several of our tales involve trading one person's pain or suffering for another person's pleasure. Negative utilitarians focus on the elimination of suffering rather than the production of pleasure. Even though pleasure contributes to human welfare, that is not our concern. As utilitarian moral agents, we should seek merely to minimize pain. Negative utilitarianism is obviously not a plausible guide to your own life. If you thought only about avoiding pain, you would never take any risks, achieve anything or enjoy any significant pleasures. However, when it comes to your impact on other people, you might think that your responsibility not to harm them is paramount. This view might particularly appeal if our utilitarianism is applied to institutions. Perhaps people are responsible for their own pleasure, while the government's role is to minimize pain and suffering.

Unfortunately, while negative utilitarianism might resolve some of our tales, it makes others worse. The demandingness complaint is that utilitarianism requires me to forego benefits for myself to alleviate the sufferings of total strangers. Negative utilitarianism is much more severe. I must give up *all pleasure* for myself to avoid the slightest pain for a complete stranger, even if that stranger otherwise enjoys a wonderful life. In other tales, negative utilitarianism makes no difference. In the trolley tale, where we must choose between an agonising death for Albert and a similar fate for ten others, negative utilitarianism offers nothing new.

Negative utilitarianism has other odd implications. If our only goal is to minimize suffering then the painless extinction of human beings (and all other creatures capable of feeling pain) would be the best possible result. In the replicas tale, a negative utilitarian will destroy everyone, and then replace them with no one. A negative utilitarian would also make choices for other people that they would never have chosen for themselves. You might be willing to undergo a certain pain to get a significant pleasure – or to avoid a painless death. As a negative utilitarian, I will try to prevent you from exercising that choice.

Rethinking distribution

Utilitarianism often favours benefits to the well-off at the expense of the worse-off. In efficient slavery, the continued affluence of free citizens is purchased with the continued suffering of slaves. Utilitarians aim at maximum total well-being, no matter how it is distributed. *Egalitarians* prefer a more equal distribution, even if total well-being is less. A *pure egalitarian* would care *only* about distribution. Pure egalitarianism is open to a seemingly decisive objection.

> **The levelling down objection to pure egalitarianism**
> You are the king of a large prosperous country. A very small number of your people suffer from an incurable disease. They live in unrelenting agony and die young. As a pure egalitarian, your only goal is to equalize the lifetime well-being of all your citizens. You cannot improve the lifetime well-being of the disease sufferers. So you equalize lifetime well-being by torturing everyone else to death in childhood.

For a pure egalitarian, it does not matter how welfare is equalized. Making happy people miserable is just as good as making miserable people happy. In practice, it is often much easier to *level down* than to level up. Some diseases cannot be cured, but anyone can be tortured to death.

Levelling down achieves equality, but provides no benefit to anyone. Torturing everyone else does nothing for the disease sufferers. Most philosophers conclude that what is really important is not equality of well-being *per se*, but the level of well-being of those who are worse-off. Levelling down is not desirable. By contrast, suppose we equalize well-being by freeing slaves. Although producers and consumers are worse-off than before, their former slaves are better-off. So this change does improve the well-being of the worse-off.

If you think levelling down is wrong – whereas freeing slaves is not – then you should reject pure egalitarianism. Equalizing well-being is not the only valuable end. If you think levelling down is not only wrong but also *pointless* – if there is no reason at all to equalize well-being in these cases – then you should reject egalitarianism altogether. But you might still be attracted to what we ordinarily think of as "egalitarian ideals". One popular alternative is *prioritarianism*. A *pure prioritarian* is *only* interested in the well-being of those who are worst-off, and not at all interested in anyone else. On this view, levelling down is neither good nor bad. I do not know of any pure prioritarians. A slightly more modest view is *lexical prioritarianism*. Everyone's well-being counts, but the well-being of those who are worst-off trumps *any* improvement in well-being for anyone else. Imagine a series of possible scenarios for two groups. (Where the numbers represent levels of well-being.)

	Group 1	Group 2
World 1	10	10
World 2	10	20
World 3	11	11

Unlike pure prioritarianism, lexical prioritarianism holds that World 2 is better than World 1. As the worse-off fare equally well in the two worlds, we look at what happens to the better-off. However, World 3 is better than World 2, as the tiny improvement for Group 1 trumps the loss for Group 2. And this is true even if Group 1 is very small and Group 2 is very large. Under lexical prioritarianism, the slightest benefit for a single badly-off person can require enormous sacrifices from everyone else. If this result disturbs us, then we might become *moderate prioritarians*. Instead of giving lexical priority to the worst-off, we merely give their interests additional weight. (Another alternative is *threshold prioritarianism*, whereby we give priority to ensuring that no one falls below a minimum acceptable level of well-being. This new concern could be either lexical or moderate.)

Opponents of all these views argue that, because they deal only with levels of welfare, neither prioritarians nor egalitarians can avoid what is really objectionable about utilitarianism. In many of our tales, prioritarianism either has no effect or makes things worse. Although torture is very bad in itself, the person being tortured may enjoy a reasonable level of overall lifetime welfare. Even if they are tortured, they will not be the worst-off person. If the bomb would kill the worst-off people, then a switch from utilitarianism to prioritarianism thus *reduces* the evil of torture. Similarly, suppose Albert has already lived a long and prosperous life. Even if you push him in front of the trolley, he will not be one of the worst-off people. Suppose the people in the trolley are the most deprived children, enjoying a rare day out. Prioritarianism now *strengthens* your obligation to push Albert! A shift to prioritarianism also definitely increases the demands of utilitarianism. If you are comparatively affluent, then you must give your own interests *even less* weight than the interests of the worst-off. None of this proves that prioritarianism is not the correct account of value. But it does suggest that, even if it is plausible in its own right, the shift to prioritarianism cannot resolve all our problems. We need to look elsewhere.

Key points

- Two key objections to utilitarianism are that it tells you to do unjust things to others (the injustice objection), and that it tells you not to do acceptable things for yourself (the demandingness objection).

- Extremists reply that morality is very demanding, and that our intuitions are unreliable.
- Some utilitarians seek to avoid these objections by arguing that, given facts about the world, utilitarianism does not permit injustices or make extreme demands.
- Other utilitarians deny that utilitarians must maximize welfare. They offer alternative accounts of value, such as egalitarianism or prioritarianism.

six

Acts, rules and institutions

Act-utilitarianism

Suppose you are a utilitarian, committed to maximizing human well-being. You have a view of well-being. What should you do? The utilitarian tradition offers four broad options: act-utilitarianism, indirect utilitarianism, rule-utilitarianism and institutional utilitarianism. This chapter examines these alternatives.

The simplest form of utilitarianism is *act-utilitarianism*. The right act is the act that produces the most well-being. This suggests that you should aim, on each occasion, to maximize welfare. This picture of utilitarians as constant calculating maximizers faces two sorts of objection: intuitive and utilitarian. The previous chapter exposed the first: act-utilitarianism is unjust, immoral, and unreasonably demanding. As we will see, one primary reason for abandoning act-utilitarianism is to avoid the injustice and demandingness objections. However, act-utilitarianism has other problems. In particular, it faces an objection on utilitarian grounds – that it is *self-defeating* because constant calculators do not maximize welfare. If our target is maximum welfare, we will sometimes do better if we do not aim directly at that target. Why is it unwise to aim directly at happiness? Because some valuable results are *calculatively elusive* – they are not available to those who deliberately aim at them. Here are some common examples.

1. *Spontaneity.* If you calculate too precisely, or focus too directly on a desired result, you will not achieve it. For instance, suppose you

are engaged in an artistic endeavour which is most valuable if performed spontaneously. You want to behave spontaneously. This result cannot be attained if you deliberately concentrate on being spontaneous.

2. *Danger.* If you are performing some dangerous task, then you risk losing your nerve if you think too much about the danger.
3. *Time is of the essence.* Some decisions must be made very quickly. If you are about to be hit by a truck, you should not wait to perform precise utilitarian calculations.
4. *Friendship.* A good friend directly pursues the interests of her friends, rather than seeking to maximize the good. Someone who only spends time with you because that maximizes overall happiness – and would abandon you immediately if she could produce more happiness elsewhere – is not a real friend. Conscious maximizers cannot either experience friendship themselves or provide the benefits of real friendship to others.
5. *Coordination problems.* Everyone must decide what side of the road to drive on. If each individual calculates the best strategy, then some will drive on the left and some on the right. The result is sub-optimal.

Many utilitarians distinguish between a *criterion of evaluation* and a *decision procedure*. Utilitarians are committed to welfare maximization as their criterion. Welfare maximization is ultimately what makes outcomes good and actions right. It may seem obvious that utilitarianism's decision procedure is: "Always seek to maximize happiness." However, the existence of calculatedly elusive benefits leads many utilitarians to deny this. Utilitarians should evaluate decision procedures the same way they evaluate anything else. The best decision procedure is whatever *procedure* maximizes happiness. This may be the simple procedure of seeking to maximize happiness, but it may not be. If some other procedure would produce more happiness, then you should follow it instead.

> There is no distinctive place for direct utilitarianism unless it is . . . a doctrine about how one should decide what to do.
> (Williams, in Smart & Williams, *Utilitarianism: For and Against*, 128)

Following Williams, some philosophers argue that criterion and decision procedure cannot come apart. James Griffin (a philosopher who is generally much more sympathetic to utilitarianism than Williams) also criticizes the relevance of a criterion of rightness which, owing to the limitations of our knowledge and psychology, could never be applied by human beings. He asks whether "a criterion that cannot be applied [is] really a criterion" (Griffin, "The Distinction between Criterion and Decision Procedure", 180–81). Defenders of the distinction reply that the utilitarian criterion can generate useful ethical advice even if we could never apply it perfectly ourselves.

Indirect utilitarianism

Indirect utilitarianism says both (a) that the right act is whatever follows from the best utilitarian decision procedure; and (b) that the best decision procedure diverges from the utilitarian criterion of rightness. Most indirect utilitarians retain act-utilitarianism as their criterion of rightness. So their distinctive claim is that act-utilitarianism is *not* the best utilitarian decision procedure.

What is the best utilitarian decision procedure? How will it differ from act-utilitarianism? Here are some differences, suggested by our earlier examples.

1. *Clear your mind.* For activities requiring spontaneity or reflex action, do not deliberate at all while performing the activity.
2. *Rules of thumb.* Many situations reflect common patterns. Follow a rule of thumb – a *prima facie* moral principle. Do not calculate where to drive – just drive on the left. Do not calculate whether to murder a random stranger – just do not kill.
3. *Timeliness.* Never deliberate too long. If time is short, then either choose the first good enough option that comes along (*satisficing*) or choose the best option of those you have time to consider (*constrained maximization*), or follow rules of thumb.
4. *Friendship.* When the interests of your friends are at stake, do not calculate. Do whatever friendship requires, so long as this does not have disastrous consequences.
5. *Conserve your resources.* As an isolated act, donating all your money to charity seems to maximize welfare. However, you will do more good over the course of your life if you keep enough money to maintain your health, hold down your job, and so on. Donating a reasonable percentage is thus the best strategy.

Indirect utilitarians use these differences from act-utilitarianism to defeat the injustice and demandingness objections. Once we shift from the isolated evaluation of particular acts to the evaluation of decision procedures or patterns of behaviour across the agent's life as a whole, we get different results in our various tales. A sheriff or other law enforcement officer who adopts the policy of never hanging or torturing the innocent will produce more happiness over the course of her life than a sheriff who is willing to hang an innocent person. Over the course of a lifetime, the hanging sheriff is likely to miscalculate, to be discovered (leading to public disgrace and loss of faith in the judicial system), or to suffer psychological trauma. These drawbacks are sufficient to outweigh the benefits an occasional hanging might produce.

A utilitarian will also do more good over the course of a lifetime if she adopts the principle of not harming or betraying her friends. This policy enables her to form genuine friendships, thus enhancing both her own happiness and that of her friends. These benefits outweigh any extra good she might do on some isolated occasion by betraying a friend. You will also do more good over the course of your life by following a career path and lifestyle that you find independently fulfilling. Giving all your money away today, or reluctantly committing to a career in banking, may produce more good in the short term, but it is unlikely to be a genuinely successful long-term strategy. Some indirect utilitarians even argue that the best overall decision procedure is simply to follow common-sense morality. This provides a clear set of well-tested rules of thumb, and easily solves many moral coordination problems, because most other people are already following common-sense morality.

These responses certainly do soften the injustice and demandingness objections. However, opponents of utilitarianism will remain unconvinced. This defence of utilitarianism seems too contingent. In the real world, it is easy to imagine cases where a particular individual might know that they would produce more happiness (over the course of their life) by following a policy of deceit or murder or torture. It may be necessary for *most* law enforcement officials not to torture, but there might be a niche in the system for one willing torturer. (The appeal to psychological costs for the torturer herself is especially problematic. It suggests that, if you happen to be someone who would enjoy torturing, then torture is the right course of action for you.) Similarly, while the happiness of you and your friends is certainly important, it is quite possible that you would produce greater happiness overall by following a policy of extreme self-sacrifice – given the vast amount of suffering and unmet need in the world.

In addition to these intuitive problems, indirect utilitarianism has also been accused of failing in utilitarian terms. It faces two particular problems: parasitism and self-defeatingness. To illustrate the first, consider a world where most people are not individual utilitarians.

The parasitic utilitarian
The lawn provides pleasure to everyone. If everyone walked on the grass it would be ruined. A sign tells everyone not to walk on the grass. Perry Parasite calculates that, if only one person walks on the grass, there will be no damage. So he walks on the grass every day, and always gets to his lecture early.

Many people find Perry's behaviour unacceptable, even though it has no negative consequences. Why should he be the only one who gets the shorter walk? More generally, an indirect utilitarian will always avoid paying tax (perhaps to donate the money to charity), and otherwise exploit the contributions of others. Indirect utilitarianism is thus unacceptable if I follow it in a world where others do not. Unfortunately, the theory fares even worse in a world where everyone else *does* follow it. Suppose everyone suddenly becomes an indirect utilitarian following Perry's decision procedure. Everyone walks on the grass and it is ruined. Even if they all realize what is happening, each of them will continue walking on the grass, as their individual walking does no harm. Indirect utilitarianism is *collectively self-defeating*. If everyone follows the theory, the result is less good – according to that theory's own criterion of evaluation – than if everyone had followed some other theory. Any utilitarian theory is collectively self-defeating if a world where everyone follows it contains less happiness than a world where most people do not.

Many philosophers, including many utilitarians, feel that no adequate moral theory can be collectively self-defeating. If a theory has a goal (such as maximizing welfare), then it should be designed to effectively and collectively promote that goal. We should always test our moral theory by asking "What if everyone did that?" (Or, as Brad Hooker suggests: "What if everyone *felt free* to do that?" The difference between the two questions arises because, for instance, a moral rule permitting everyone to use a public park may be perfectly acceptable, even though it would be disastrous if everyone actually did use the park at the same time.) This thought leads to rule-utilitarianism.

Rule-utilitarianism

The basic rule-utilitarian idea is simple. Instead of individual decision procedures, we evaluate codes of moral rules. The *ideal code* is the set of rules where the consequences of everyone following them would be better than the consequences of everyone following any other set of rules. We then assess acts *indirectly*. The right act is the act called for by the ideal code.

Rule-utilitarianism has considerable intuitive appeal. A serious problem for utilitarianism is that a lone individual can often do more good by violating common-sense moral rules than by following them: walking on the grass to get to a lecture, murdering to prevent more murders, torturing the terrorist's innocent grandmother to avert a catastrophe, and so on. Rule-utilitarianism avoids these counter-examples: things go better if we all follow common-sense moral rules than if we *all* feel free to violate them. In recent decades, as moral philosophers have become more interested in intuitive plausibility, rule-utilitarianism has attracted more attention.

The leading contemporary rule-utilitarian is Brad Hooker, who formulates the theory as follows.

Hooker's rule-utilitarianism
An act is wrong if and only if it is forbidden by the code of rules whose internalization by the overwhelming majority of everyone everywhere in each new generation has maximum expected value in terms of well-being (with some priority for the worst-off). The calculation of a code's expected value includes all costs of getting the code internalized. If in terms of expected value two or more codes are better than the rest but equal to one another, the one closest to conventional morality determines what acts are wrong.

(Brad Hooker, *Ideal Code, Real World*, 32)

Rule-utilitarianism was rejected through most of the twentieth century. The strongest attacks came from other utilitarians – arguing that rule-utilitarianism cannot be a useful distinctive utilitarian theory. Either it is useless, or it is indistinguishable from act-utilitarianism (or indirect utilitarianism), or it is incoherent. These controversies set the scene for contemporary rule-utilitarianism.

The most basic objection to rule-utilitarianism is the *rule worship objection*. Rule-utilitarianism begins with the standard utilitarian commitment to maximize happiness. Yet it then tells us to follow certain rules, even where this will obviously not produce the best possible consequences. Real utilitarians, it is argued, should use rules only as strategies, decision procedures or rules of thumb. "What sort of utilitarians are you?" act-utilitarians say to rule-utilitarians, accusing them of irrational "rule worship". (This is also sometimes known as the *incoherence objection* – the thought being that it is incoherent to choose rules on the basis of consequences and then refuse to depart from those rules when this promises better consequences.)

This objection has been very influential. Many rule-utilitarians deny that they are committed to maximizing happiness, and seek alternative defences of their theory. Rule-utilitarianism is now often defended primarily by reference to the intuitive appeal of its particular judgements and moral rules, or by reference to general moral ideals other than a bare commitment to maximum welfare. One very common defence of rule-utilitarianism sees it as the most natural way to develop the moral ideas underlying the common accusation: "What if everyone did that?" These include universalizability and fairness. This argument is comparative. Other moral theories provide competing accounts of these moral ideals. Rule-utilitarians claim theirs is the most plausible. This rule-utilitarian idea of fairness relates to a fair distribution of the demands of morality, not to a fair distribution of goods or opportunities. The thought is that it is unfair for a moral theory to require some to do more *because* others are doing less – as both act-utilitarianism and indirect utilitarianism do. These theories place extreme demands on you because others do not behave as they should.

Theoretical defences of any theory often go together with practical arguments. One test of a theory's account of a general moral ideal is whether it enables us to make plausible judgements in particular cases. A moral theory generating absurd particular results is unlikely to have accurately captured the essence of our general moral ideals. The best test of rule-utilitarianism's account of fairness is whether the theory deals effectively with the injustice and demandingness objections. But before we ask this, we must first deal with two other common objections to rule-utilitarianism. The first is in some ways the reverse of the collective self-defeating objection to indirect utilitarianism, while the second is a difficulty rule-utilitarians confront when attempting to deal with the first.

1. *The partial compliance objection.* Because it only asks what would happen if everybody followed a rule, rule-utilitarianism cannot

cope with real life situations of partial compliance, where not everyone follows the correct rule. Here are two common examples.

Sub-optimal coordination. In your country people drive on the left. You decide it would be better if everyone drove on the right. As a rule-utilitarian, you start driving on the right, even though everyone else keeps driving on the left. The results are not pleasant.

Dealing with wrong-doers. Rule-utilitarians want their ideal code to include familiar prohibitions on stealing, murder, breaking promises, lying, torture, and so on. (This is the main reason why rule-utilitarianism is more intuitively appealing than indirect utilitarianism.) However, if everyone obeyed those prohibitions, there would be no need for rules telling us how to deal with thieves, murderers, liars or torturers. In a world of full compliance, everyone would always be perfectly honest, never lock their doors, never check their change, always lend money to anyone who asked for it, and so on. Anyone following *this* ideal code of rules in the real world will soon look pretty stupid.

2. *The collapse objection.* Some opponents argue that rule-utilitarianism collapses into *act*-utilitarianism. Things will go best overall if everyone follows the single rule: "Always maximize happiness." So the ideal code consists of this one rule. A more moderate accusation is that rule-utilitarianism collapses into *indirect* utilitarianism. Even if the ideal code is not the simple rule "always maximize happiness", it will be identical to the best utilitarian decision procedure for an isolated individual. Most proponents of this objection are defenders of act- or indirect utilitarianism. Their objection is not that rule-utilitarianism is false, but that it is redundant. Rule-utilitarianism is a needlessly complicated version of act- or indirect utilitarianism.

The real challenge for rule-utilitarians is to avoid both objections simultaneously, as replies to one objection often make the other worse. Against the partial compliance objection, rule-utilitarians have two strategies: to introduce disaster-avoidance clauses or to restrict the scope of rule-utilitarianism. Both strategies threaten to collapse into act- or indirect utilitarianism.

Rule-utilitarians often deal with sub-optimal coordination by adding *disaster avoidance clauses* to the ideal code: "Do *x*, unless doing *x* will lead to great disaster, in which case do *y* (where *y* avoids disaster)." Your ideal road rule would be: "Drive on the right, unless everyone else is driving on the left, in which case drive on the left."

But now suppose we add a new clause, not only to avert terrible disasters, but every time a rule produces a sub-optimal result. Each new clause improves the ideal code. But eventually we end up with a very complicated set of rules identical in practice to act-utilitarianism. ("Do *x* unless doing *x* will lead to a worse result, otherwise do *y*.") We then replace those complicated rules with a simple rule exactly identical to act-utilitarianism. Rule-utilitarianism has collapsed into act-utilitarianism.

To deal with wrong-doers (our second partial compliance problem), rule-utilitarians restrict the scope of their theory, in one of two ways.

- *Global imperfect compliance.* Instead of asking what would happen if *everyone always* followed a code, we ask what would happen if *most* people *usually* followed it. If some people sometimes steal or lie, a code with sensible rules for dealing with thieves and liars will beat one without.
- *Case-by-case non-compliance.* We assess each rule in isolation. To deal with theft, we assume there are some thieves (or, at least, some potential thieves) and seek the optimal response from the rest of us.

Both solutions face problems. The global option is arbitrary. How many is "most"? The case-by-case option is threatened by the fact that many current ethical problems are due, not to the bad actions of the few, but to the inaction of the many. Consider a simple hypothetical case. Through no fault of their own, some people in a poor country face starvation or famine. One pound from each affluent person in the world would remove the problem. The ideal code says everyone should give a pound. If everyone did as they should, you would only need to give a pound. Unfortunately, almost no one does. You want to know what you should do. Under case-by-case non-compliance, you ask which rule would produce the most happiness if it were followed by everyone – *except* those whose non-compliance creates the problem. So you ask what rule would be best if followed by you and almost no one else. Your rule-utilitarianism has now collapsed into indirect utilitarianism.

To avoid these two objections, rule-utilitarians seek a middle ground between overly simplistic rules and infinitely complex ones. Many contemporary formulations of rule-utilitarianism are driven by the need to differentiate the theory from indirect utilitarianism. Why will rule-utilitarians not want the same code as indirect utilitarians? We explore this question using the injustice and demandingness objections.

Rule-utilitarianism reflects a picture of morality as a task given, not to isolated individual rational agents (as in act- or indirect utilitarianism), but to a particular *community* of *human beings*. The questions it responds to are: "What if *we* did that?", and "How should *we* live?" We are choosing a moral code to govern our community, and asking what code we should teach the next generation.

One striking feature of humans is our fallibility. Perhaps act-utilitarianism would be the ideal code for perfect utilitarian calculators. But human beings are not perfect utilitarian calculators, nor should they try to be. Specific moral rules correct specific human failings. Because we tend to think we know what is best for other people, we need to be told to respect the autonomy of others. Because we naturally favour our own interests, and those of our nearest and dearest, we need to be told to be more impartial. But because we cannot be completely impartial, we must also be allowed some partiality.

This focus on community and fallibility underlies the rule-utilitarian response to the injustice and demandingness objections. The consequences of everyone following a policy of torture or murder would be disastrous. If everyone felt free to murder, torture or betray their friends whenever the utilitarian calculations deemed it desirable, no one would enjoy any security at all. A single doctor murdering patients to provide organs for transplant might create an isolated scandal. But if all doctors followed that policy, then no one would ever visit a doctor or enter a hospital. This is the rule-utilitarian response to the injustice objections.

The response to the demandingness objections is similar. Sidgwick observed that human beings cannot feel a strong concern for everyone. If everyone tried to be perfectly impartial, then no one would feel strong concern for anyone else. Things go better overall if people give priority to themselves and their friends and family, rather than trying to impartially maximize the happiness of everyone. A world where everyone thought only of others would be chaotic and unproductive. A small contribution from each affluent person would be more than sufficient to alleviate hunger and poverty, and meet all the needs of everyone in the world. A world where everyone devoted considerable attention to themselves but also made a reasonable contribution to charity would be a happier and wealthier world than one where everyone obsessively tried to improve the lives of others. In general, people's lives go better if they devote themselves to projects they care about.

The rule-utilitarian response to the injustice and demandingness objections is similar to the indirect utilitarian solution. Both focus on the negative consequences of pursuing a policy of torture or murder or self-sacrifice, and claim that the positive benefits of these policies cannot outweigh the costs. However, the rule-utilitarian case is stronger for several reasons.

1. *Compound negative effects.* Many social institutions require a high level of trust and cooperation, but not absolute faith in the behaviour of others. Such institutions can survive the defection or non-compliance of a single isolated individual, but would collapse if people in general did not comply. For instance, public faith in the judicial or medical systems can survive one or two rotten apples, but could not survive if corrupt officials or murdering doctors were the norm.

2. *Publicity effects.* A single utilitarian individual might be able to pursue a policy of murder or torture in secrecy, but it is hard to imagine a world where *everyone* pursues such a policy without this being common knowledge. Also, while a single utilitarian fanatic might have no impact on public confidence, public confidence is impossible in a world full of utilitarian fanatics.

3. *The benefits of parasitism.* Many of the benefits produced when a single utilitarian follows a policy of murder or torture, or when they devote all their time, energy and money to charity, are only possible because that individual lives in a society where everyone else follows the rules of common-sense morality. In the real world, where most people are probably *too* partial, a lone individual can do a great deal of good. By contrast, the ideal code would leave far less unmet need. The benefits per person of following very demanding policies are thus reduced if everyone is following those policies.

4. *The costs of inculcation.* Some modern rule-utilitarians – most prominently Hooker – argue that the appropriate test for rules is not what would happen if everyone *followed* them, but instead what would happen if everyone *accepted* them. We want our code of rules to capture an ideal set of attitudes to morality, not just a pattern of behaviour. Rules that cannot be accepted, cannot really be followed – in the morally important sense. And, before it can be accepted by a society of human beings, a code of rules must first be successfully *taught* to them. Rules that cannot be taught, cannot be either accepted or followed. Hooker then argues that indirect utilitarianism is too difficult to follow and too psychologically alienating for human beings to accept. Trying

to teach that code would not maximize happiness. A very partial or demanding rule might be possible for an isolated individual but could not be easily taught to a whole generation. Rule-utilitarianism trades off the desire to maximize happiness against the need for a teachable code. The more complex, demanding or counter-intuitive a code, the higher the rate of (a) failures to learn the code at all, (b) failures to learn particular rules, or (c) failures to follow the code.

5. *Self-defeatingness.* By definition, the ideal code does the best job of promoting happiness if everyone follows it. Rule-utilitarianism, whatever its other faults, cannot be collectively self-defeating. If indirect utilitarianism *is* collectively self-defeating, then it cannot be identical to rule-utilitarianism.

In the rule-utilitarian context, policies of murder, torture, betrayal, or extreme self-sacrifice thus involve greater costs and lesser benefits than in the indirect utilitarian context. This suggests that rule-utilitarianism is better able to justify common-sense prohibitions on murder and torture, or common-sense permissions to favour one's friends or oneself. Rule-utilitarians will choose a less impartial and less demanding decision procedure than indirect utilitarians.

Rule-utilitarianism is thus distinct from indirect utilitarianism. But is it sufficiently distinct? Is it intuitively plausible? Even if we know that the ideal code does not coincide with indirect utilitarianism, do we know what that code is? Is rule-utilitarianism the right response to the value of community?

Suppose we agree that utilitarians will not go around torturing the innocent, murdering their patients, betraying their friends or bankrupting themselves for charity. This is not sufficient to prove that utilitarians behave properly. We also need to know exactly how a rule-utilitarian sheriff or doctor would behave. How much of a real friend could a rule-utilitarian be? Even if the theory is not as demanding as indirect utilitarianism, it might still be extremely demanding. For a taste of the complexities here, we briefly consider the rule-utilitarian response to famine. Which of the following rules do you think the ideal code should include?

Rule A. Give 1 per cent of your income to charity.
Rule B. Give x per cent of your income to charity, where x is between 0 and 100.
Rule C. Give all of your income to charity.

Suppose, along with many contemporary rule-utilitarians, we agree that things go best if everyone gives something like 10 per cent. Unfortunately, our task is not nearly finished. Rule-utilitarianism must guide us in the real world. We need to know, not only how people behave in the ideal society, but also what rules they are following. Many different rules might produce the same patterns of behaviour under full compliance, but very different results under partial compliance. Here are a few examples.

Rule B1. Give 10 per cent of your income to charity, irrespective of what other people do.

Rule B2. Give 10 per cent to charity if most other people will do so; otherwise give nothing, as you cannot remove poverty.

Rule B3. Give 10 per cent to charity if enough others will do so; otherwise give more because there is more suffering. (There are many possible versions of this rule, depending on how much more you should give.)

Rule B4. Give 10 per cent to charity if enough others will do so; otherwise maximize utility.

If rule-utilitarians cannot tell us exactly which rule to follow, then their theory is of no practical use. We return to these issues in Chapter 8.

Institutional utilitarianism

The strength of utilitarianism, the problem to which it is a truly compelling solution, is as a guide to public rather than private conduct. There, virtually all its vices – all the things that make us wince in recommending it as a code of personal morality – loom instead as considerable virtues.

(Goodin, *Utilitarianism as a Public Philosophy*, 8)

Twentieth-century discussions of utilitarianism focused on act-utilitarianism. The standard objections to utilitarianism (such as the injustice and demandingness objections) are really aimed at act-utilitarianism. This suggests that some classical utilitarians would not have been bothered by those objections, as they depart from act-utilitarianism in two key ways: they reject consequentialism and they focus on institutions. The first of these departures is examined in the next chapter. This section examines the second.

Institutional utilitarianism is the view that the best political, legislative or social institutions are those that produce the greatest total well-being. This view is prominent in the writings of the classical utilitarians. Bentham focused primarily on institutions. Mill, although he wrote his *Utilitarianism* from the perspective of the individual agent, was also very interested in institutions. These classical utilitarians sought to design public institutions that would maximize human happiness. In contemporary moral philosophy, institutional utilitarianism is usually treated as a sub-topic within rule-utilitarianism – if it is discussed at all. The reason is not philosophical or utilitarian, but instead reflects administrative divisions within universities. Rule-utilitarianism is *moral philosophy*, taught in philosophy departments; while institutional utilitarianism is *political philosophy*, often taught in departments of politics, government, economics or law. In political philosophy, utilitarianism has largely fallen out of favour due to attacks by Rawls and Robert Nozick. (Rawls' attack was examined in Chapter 5. Nozick's attack begins with his experience machine (Chapter 4), and is also linked to his libertarianism.) Furthermore, the prevailing ethos in contemporary political philosophy regards it as largely independent of moral philosophy. Political philosophy deals with issues that arise precisely because, in modern liberal societies, citizens must find ways to live together despite the fact that they cannot agree on controversial moral questions. This immediately places utilitarianism at a disadvantage, as it rejects any sharp divide between moral and political philosophy. No magic line separates moral rules from political institutions, or principles of morality from principles of justice. Any division must be justified on the grounds of its contribution to human welfare.

As utilitarians, we should include institutional utilitarianism under rule-utilitarianism. Considering rules and institutions together can help to resolve some objections to utilitarianism. Both act- and indirect utilitarianism take political institutions for granted, and ask how I should respond to them. Rule-utilitarians must re-evaluate all institutions, as a complete moral code would tell us what institutions to create as well as how to respond to existing institutions. Sometimes the failings of utilitarianism in individual morality are its strengths when we come to institutions. For instance, institutional utilitarians have straightforward replies to the injustice and demandingness objections. If we are designing institutions for a human society, then we want those institutions to be public and accountable, for the reasons identified by Bentham. So the best judicial institutions will discourage sheriffs from hanging or torturing the innocent, and the best hospital system will discourage doctors from murdering their patients. Similarly, while partiality to oneself and one's friends is a virtue in private life, it is a sign of corruption in public officials. When we are designing institutions, the impartiality of utilitarianism is an asset. Another significant advantage of institutional utilitarianism is its ability to cope with uncertainty, as we shall see in Chapter 8.

Key points

- Utilitarianism can focus on acts, decision procedures, rules or institutions.
- Act-utilitarianism says the right action maximizes well-being.
- Indirect utilitarians defend decision procedures other than act-utilitarianism.
- Rule-utilitarianism says the right action follows from rules that would maximize well-being if everyone followed them.
- Rule-utilitarians must show that their theory does not collapse into act-utilitarianism.
- Rule-utilitarians argue that their theory is closer to common-sense morality than act-utilitarianism.
- Institutional utilitarianism says the best institutions maximize total well-being.

seven

Consequentialism

This chapter focuses on a feature of utilitarianism that is attracting considerable attention in current moral theory: the fact that utilitarianism assumes that the only rational response to value is to promote it. In current discussions, this *consequentialist* principle is often taken to be the defining feature of the whole utilitarian tradition, to the extent that utilitarianism is presented as one form of consequentialism. Utilitarianism *is* consequentialism (morality promotes value) *plus* welfarism (value is aggregate human welfare).

Opponents of consequentialism argue that, unless they abandon the basic consequentialist idea, utilitarians cannot hope to avoid either the demandingness or injustice objections. Any theory telling us to maximize value will make unreasonable demands and permit appalling injustices – no matter what theory of value it incorporates, or whether it seeks to maximize value individually (as do act- and indirect utilitarianism) or collectively (as do rule- and institutional utilitarianism). The shift in emphasis from utilitarianism to consequentialism thus raises several questions. What is the consequentialist response to value? Is it unreasonably demanding or otherwise counter-intuitive? What are the alternative responses to value? How does consequentialism relate to utilitarianism?

What is consequentialism?

The basic point of consequentialism is that the appropriate response to value is to promote it. If you think x is good, then you should try to increase the amount of x in the world. If happiness is good, you should maximize happiness. If chocolate-eating is the only value, you should promote chocolate-eating. Consequentialism thus builds on the simple thought that morality is all about making the world a better place. Its most strident defenders take consequentialism to be true by definition. This view was advanced by G. E. Moore, a student of Sidgwick's who argued that "x is right" simply *means* "x best promotes the good". (Moore explicitly rejected the utilitarian account of value. He was thus the first prominent non-utilitarian consequentialist.) As we saw in Chapter 3, this is also the view of Hare, who offers a definitely utilitarian analysis – "x is right" means "x maximizes preference satisfaction." Anyone who is not a consequentialist just does not understand moral language! On a more modest formulation of this view, while non-consequentialist moral theories are not actually contradictory, the only *rational* way to respond to any value is to promote it. If happiness is valuable, then the only rational course of action is to maximize happiness. Consequentialism is thus the most rational moral theory, always telling us to promote value.

Some consequentialists draw an analogy between moral rationality and individual (self-interested) rationality. Just as a rational agent seeks to maximize her own expected utility, so a moral agent should seek to maximize the well-being of all agents. Consequentialism is thus rational and impartial. Hare's derivation is a classic example of this style of argument. Others see consequentialism as a natural account of the central moral values of impartiality and equality, as it treats all agents perfectly equally and is thus perfectly impartial. Other consequentialists appeal to the theoretical virtue of simplicity. Promotion is sometimes a rational response to value. (If health is valuable, then it is obviously good to promote people's health.) So the simplest moral theory will recommend promotion as a universal response to value.

These arguments are all highly controversial. Consequentialist accounts of rationality, impartiality, equality and simplicity have all been challenged, as has the underlying assumption that an acceptable moral theory must be rational, or egalitarian, or impartial, or simple. The main intuitive objections to consequentialism are the demandingness and injustice objections. We have already dealt with these in detail for utilitarianism. We must now ask if consequentialists who are *not* utilitarians fare any better.

Non-utilitarian consequentialism

Separating utilitarianism from consequentialism opens up two new options: utilitarianism without consequentialism and consequentialism without utilitarianism. We explore each in turn. Can consequentialists avoid the injustice and demandingness objections by rejecting utilitarian values? We have already looked at some non-standard versions of utilitarianism, such as prioritarianism and egalitarianism. We could regard these as non-utilitarian consequentialist theories, as they maximize something other than total human well-being. We saw in Chapter 5 that these theories do not avoid our two sets of objections. In Chapter 4, we briefly examined other departures from (or extensions of) utilitarian values, accommodating animal welfare and the intrinsic value of natural beauty. Whatever its other merits, a consequentialist theory based on these values will still fail to avoid our two objections. The introduction of these new values clearly makes consequentialism even more demanding, as I will now be required to make enormous sacrifices, not only to provide benefits to other humans, but also to save trees, whales or wetlands. The injustice objection is also exacerbated for the same reason. For instance, could a consequentialist sheriff now find himself having to execute an innocent person to prevent a mob of anti-environmentalists from hunting (innocent) foxes?

A more promising alternative is to attach intrinsic disvalue directly to injustice. This gives consequentialists a clear reply to the injustice objection – the sheriff does the wrong thing because he fails to minimize injustice. This strategy faces two problems. Unless injustice is our only value, it will often be outweighed by other considerations, such as welfare. The sheriff might still maximize *total* value by executing the innocent person. On the other hand, a moral theory where justice is the *only* value will produce strange results elsewhere. When happiness is at stake and justice is not, such a theory will be completely silent. We could seek a more complex value theory, where both happiness and justice are valuable, but where (the slightest amount of) justice always trumps (any amount of) happiness. Justice has *lexical priority* over happiness. No matter how many lives are at stake, the sheriff always maximizes value by refusing to hang an innocent person. However, this lexical view will seem implausible to anyone sympathetic to the utilitarian tradition. Do we really want to say that a world where millions of people live flourishing lives and there are some isolated injustices is worse *overall* than a world where millions of people are terribly miserable but there is no injustice?

A broader problem for any attempt to use the value of justice to defeat the injustice objection is that, if our aim is to maximize justice (or minimize injustice), then we may often find ourselves committing one injustice to prevent a greater wrong. If the riot is itself an injustice, then the sheriff must still hang Bob. And you must still torture the terrorist's child, as a terrorist attack is a very great injustice.

It seems we can only avoid our objections by revising consequentialism. Suppose we begin with a theory I shall call *simple consequentialism*. This theory tells each agent, on each occasion, to choose the act that maximizes impartial value. Simple consequentialism has five principal features: *individualism, directness, act focus, maximization* and *impartiality*. We can depart from simple consequentialism by varying one or more of these five basic features. Earlier chapters explored variations to the first three factors. Should value be promoted individually or collectively? Should agents aim to promote value directly or indirectly? Should our focus be on acts, or on decision procedures, or rules, or institutions?

We now briefly address the other two variations – departures from maximization or impartiality. The reason we did not deal with these objections earlier is largely historical. While the first three departures from consequentialism are all well represented in the classic literature on utilitarianism itself, these two new variations have only come to prominence more recently, and in relation to consequentialism in general. Unfortunately, while these two new variants may weaken the demandingness objection, they both make consequentialism even more unjust. This will lead us to consider non-consequentialist responses to value.

Satisficing consequentialism

Consequentialism is so demanding because it always requires the best possible result. It is not enough to produce good consequences; you must maximize. It is not sufficient to save some lives; you must save as many as possible. So the easiest way to make consequentialism less demanding is to abandon maximization. Perhaps we should *promote* value without *maximizing* it. The best known example in contemporary moral philosophy is Michael Slote's *satisficing consequentialism*. Slote argues that consequentialist morality should be analogous to economic rationality. Satisficing consequentialism is the moral analogue of a familiar economic notion. A *satisficing* firm takes the first good enough offer that comes along, rather than waiting indefinitely for a perfect offer. Similarly, moral agents must produce a *good enough outcome*, but they need not produce the best.

Many consequentialists regard satisficing as a plausible *decision procedure*: the best way to maximize value in the long term is to aim at good enough results, rather than always striving to produce the best possible results. However, our discussion in Chapter 6 suggests that this indirect satisficing alone cannot defeat the demandingness objection, as any theory ultimately committed to maximizing value will still be very demanding. Slote's response is to go further. He presents satisficing as a *criterion of rightness*. You are always permitted to produce a good enough result, even if you know exactly how to produce much more value. We might say that Slote's satisficing is *blatant*, not merely *strategic*. If we set a low enough threshold for a result to count as "good enough", then it seems we can easily use blatant moral satisficing to avoid unreasonable demands. Unfortunately, satisficing consequentialism is open to a number of objections. It does not really solve the demandingness objection, and it makes the injustice objection much worse. Each objection begins from a simple tale.

The dead warrior
Eric, a great warrior, dies and arrives in Valhalla. The gods reward him by offering to grant any wish he makes. Eric asks that his family and their descendants be made "fairly well-off" for the rest of their lives. The gods ask him if he means as well-off as possible. "No", Eric replies, "I think fairly well-off would be good enough." Has Eric done the right thing?

This tale is adapted from one presented by Slote, who endorses Eric's choice. Eric does nothing wrong by not requesting that his family be made as well-off as possible. It is enough that they will be fairly well-off. However, Slote ignores another, more serious, way that Eric satisfices. Eric requests benefits *only* for his family, when he could have considered everyone else in the world, especially those living in poverty or misery. A result may be good enough in two distinct ways. On the *individual interpretation*, a result is good enough overall only if it is good enough for *each* person who is affected. On the *collective interpretation*, a result can be good enough *overall*, even though there are some particular individuals for whom that result is *not good* enough.

Unfortunately, neither interpretation is satisfactory. A theory requiring outcomes that are good enough under the *individual* interpretation would still be *very* demanding. Even if you have saved 100 people from starvation, you must still continue until no one is starving – no matter what the cost to yourself. A theory requiring only a good enough outcome under the *collective* interpretation will be either too demanding or too undemanding, depending on its definition of "good enough". If we are to avoid extreme demands in everyday life, we must allow that saving 100 people from starvation is good enough. But now suppose I choose to save only 100 people from starvation, even though I could have saved 200 people at no extra cost to myself. Can I stop once I have saved 100 people, on the grounds that I have "done enough good"? The problem with satisficing consequentialism is that it takes no account of the cost to the agent. As a result, whichever interpretation we choose, we will end up with demands that are unreasonably high in some cases and unreasonably low in others.

The trolley case
Mary stands on a bridge over a railway track. A trolley carrying ten people passes under the bridge. Unless stopped, the trolley will plunge over a cliff. Also on the bridge are two sand bags (one heavier than the other), and Bob (an innocent bystander). Mary knows that ten people will perish unless she acts. Mary can stop the trolley by causing any of these three objects to fall on the tracks. Mary is a brilliant engineer, able to predict all of the following consequences. If Mary throws the heavier sand bag, then the trolley stops. All ten people are saved. If Mary throws the lighter sand bag, then the trolley teeters on the edge. Two people fall out and die. If Mary throws Bob, then Bob tries to avoid the trolley. It still kills him, but it only just stops in time. One person falls out and dies. Finally, if Mary shoots Bob, then the trolley runs over Bob's body and stops earlier. All ten are saved. What should Mary do? (This tale is based on an example made famous (among philosophers) by Philippa Foot.)

It seems obvious that Mary ought to throw the heavier sand bag, thereby saving all ten people without endangering Bob. However, suppose throwing the lighter bag produces a good enough outcome. So satisficing consequentialism must permit Mary to throw it instead. (If Mary is *not* allowed to throw the lighter bag – presumably because saving eight lives is not "good enough" – then satisficing consequentialism will be extremely demanding in other situations.) She must also be permitted to perform any other action which produces at least as good a result. So pushing Bob off the bridge is also morally acceptable. This is bad enough, but there is worse to come. Shooting Bob produces an even better result. Therefore, if Mary is permitted to throw the lighter bag, then she must also be permitted to shoot bystander Bob!

Partial consequentialism

Some opponents argue that the stringency of consequentialism stems from its commitment to impartiality. So we should depart from simple consequentialism by allowing agents to give particular weight to their own interests or values. We will explore one variation developed by Samuel Scheffler. We begin with a contrast between two different perspectives: an *impersonal perspective*, where the welfare of all individuals is given exactly equal weight; and a *personal perspective*, where you give extra weight to your own interests and projects, and to the welfare of those close to you. A central question in moral philosophy is: what is the relationship between these two perspectives? Here are four simple answers.

1. Only the impersonal perspective is morally significant. (Simple consequentialism takes this view.)
2. Only the personal perspective is morally significant. (This would give us an egocentric morality.)
3. Both perspectives are morally important, but each has its own separate domain: an area of life in which it is to dominate, to the exclusion of the other perspective. (We might call this a *compartmentalist* moral theory.)
4. Both perspectives are morally important, not just within a limited sphere, but over the agent's life as a whole. The two perspectives must be *balanced* against one another. (We might call this an *integrationist* moral theory.)

Scheffler's *hybrid view* is integrationist. Under simple consequentialism, the weight an agent is allowed to give to her own personal projects is in strict proportion to their impersonal value. You should only pursue your hobby of grass counting if the well-being you receive is greater than the total well-being you could generate for others by acting differently. Scheffler departs from simple consequentialism by endorsing *agent-centred prerogatives*. These allow "each agent to assign certain proportionately greater weight to his own interests than to the interests of other people" (Scheffler, *The Rejection of Consequentialism*, 20). Scheffler provides the following explication.

> Suppose, in other words, that each agent were allowed to give M times more weight to his own interests than to the interests of anyone else. This would mean that an agent was permitted to perform his preferred act (call it P), provided that there was no alternative A open to him, such that (1) A would produce a better overall outcome than P, as judged from an impersonal standpoint which gives equal weight to everyone's interests, and (2) the total net loss to others of his doing P rather than A was more than M times as great as the net loss to him of doing A rather than P.
>
> (Scheffler, "Prerogatives without Restrictions", 378)

Scheffler distinguishes two features of common-sense morality that are *not* found in simple consequentialism: agent-centred prerogatives *allowing* us not to promote the good, and *agent-centred restrictions preventing* us from producing the best outcome – for instance, "Never kill the innocent" forbids killing the innocent even when doing so would produce the best possible consequences. The hybrid view incorporates agent-centred prerogatives, but not agent-centred restrictions. It is a middle road between simple consequentialism and common-sense morality. By setting M sufficiently high, the hybrid view easily avoids the demandingness objection. The hybrid view also respects one key aspect of the separateness of persons – it does not require the agent to treat her own welfare the same as everyone else's.

Unfortunately, the hybrid view makes the injustice objections worse. Consider two situations where the pursuit of my projects requires a large sum of money. In the first, I do not have enough money, so I kill my uncle to inherit £10,000. In the other, I already have £10,000, and I do not give it to charity to save a stranger's life. For the hybrid view, these two cases are morally equivalent. An agent-centred prerogative can allow me to leave distant strangers to die if and only if it also permits me to kill. If prerogatives are to be any use at all, they must (at least sometimes) allow me to spend my money on myself rather than on saving the lives of others. "Allowing to die" must sometimes be permitted. So I must sometimes be allowed to kill to advance my own personal projects – even at the expense of the general good. The hybrid view also permits many other injustices, as the following tales demonstrate.

> **Amy and Bob's dilemma**
> Amy, Bob and Clare are sitting in their living room. A ravenous space alien is about to devour Clare. Amy can chop off her own arm and throw it to the alien – distracting it while Clare escapes and Bob uses his ray gun to vaporize the alien. What should Amy and Bob do?

Let us assume that Amy is permitted to sacrifice her arm, but she is not required to do so. (If it does require this, then the hybrid view is very demanding.) But *Bob* is also allowed to maximize the good. So Bob can sacrifice Amy's arm without her consent, if this is the only way he can save Clare. Is this plausible?

> **The partnership**
> Ant and Bee are friends. At time *t*, Ant's agent-centred prerogative permits her to embark on a cooperative venture with Bee. Between *t* and *t*+1, both Ant and Bee invest a great deal of time and effort in their project, all of which will be wasted if either abandons it. What should Ant do?

At *t*+1, Ant is permitted to continue with the project, assuming she still values it. However, Ant is allowed to abandon the joint project to maximize impersonal value. Ant is also permitted to abandon the cooperative project to pursue some new personal project of her own – even to enter into a new cooperative project with Spider, a sworn enemy of Bee's. This seems very unfair on Bee.

Both satisficing consequentialism and the hybrid view reduce the demands of consequentialism by limiting our obligation to promote the good. However, because neither theory incorporates any restrictions in addition to its prerogatives, there is nothing to stop you using your freedom to torture, murder or betray your friends. Both theories make the *injustice* objections even worse, even if they do avoid the *demandingness* objections. Of course, simple consequentialism also permits many morally dubious actions. But it only does so if you are aiming to maximize the good. By contrast, our two moderate consequentialist theories give you a licence to murder, torture or betray in pursuit of your own personal projects, even when the result does not maximize human happiness overall.

Another option worth exploring would bring in indirect utilitarianism – retaining traditional utilitarianism as our criterion of rightness, but offering satisficing consequentialism or the hybrid view as our decision procedure. Consequentialists often respond to the injustice and demandingness objections by combining different strategies in this way.

Honouring value

Opponents of consequentialism join with defenders of simple consequentialism in rejecting both satisficing consequentialism and the hybrid view as unsatisfactory compromises. Options without constraints are untenable. Yet a consequentialist rationale for constraints or restrictions is difficult to find. The whole point of a restriction is that it prevents you from doing x even if your aim is to minimize the amount of x that is done. You cannot commit one murder to prevent several other murders. How can we make sense of this if promotion is the only rational response to value?

If consequentialists cannot justify restrictions, then perhaps we must build non-consequentialist responses to value into the foundations of moral theory. Our ultimate aim is to ask if these non-consequentialist foundations can be combined with utilitarianism. However, we begin with explicitly non-utilitarian theories, as most contemporary non-consequentialists are not utilitarian.

In the last two hundred years of moral philosophy, the promotion of value has most often been contrasted with a response known as *honouring* or *respecting* value. Sometimes the appropriate way to respond to the fact that something is valuable is not to seek to produce as much of it as possible, but to respect the instances of that value that already exist, whenever you encounter them. Honouring is especially thought to be an appropriate response to the kind of value found in human beings. If you think human life is valuable, you should respect human life – for instance, by never taking a human life, even to save several other lives. If you push Albert in front of the trolley, or if you hang an innocent person to prevent a riot, then you dishonour that person's humanity.

The importance of honouring the value of humanity was the foundation of the moral theory of the great eighteenth-century German philosopher Immanuel Kant. Over the last two centuries, Kantian ethics has been the principal theoretical opponent of utilitarianism, at least in academic philosophical circles. Kant deliberately presents his theory in opposition to early British expressions of utilitarianism. What is valuable about human beings is not that we can feel pleasure or pain, but that we have a capacity for rational autonomy – the ability to freely live our own lives in accordance with the moral law. Because it recognizes the value of rational autonomy, the moral law tells me always to respect human freedom and rationality, both in myself and in other people. I should always treat each person as an end-in-themselves, not merely as a means to my own ends.

It is important to note that Kant does not deny that you can use another person as a means. You simply cannot treat them *only* as a means. The classic example is my dealings with a shopkeeper. My motivation for entering this particular shop probably has nothing to do with respect. I am simply pursuing my own interests. If I could gain the same goods at the same price by putting money into a vending machine or purchasing over the internet from an automated computer, then I would. However, having chosen to use shopkeepers rather than vending machines as the means to my own ends, I must interact with shopkeepers in a way that acknowledges that, unlike a machine, they are rational agents. I should thus bargain honestly and courteously, rather than seeking to steal, threaten or cheat. If I cannot use shopkeepers as means without violating respect, then I should not use them at all.

Murder obviously fails to respect someone as an end-in-themselves, as it deprives them of any future capacity for rational choice or freedom. Less obviously, lying is just as strictly forbidden. Kant focuses on my reasons for lying – on the *maxim* I would be following if I told a lie. If I tell someone a lie, it is presumably because I want them to do something that I know they will not do if they know the truth. For instance, suppose Albert is too strong for you to push him in front of the trolley. You know that if you told Albert the truth and asked him to sacrifice his life, he would refuse. So you trick Albert into walking in front of the trolley, by telling him there is treasure buried under the railway line and that no trolleys are approaching. Here is a more mundane example. Suppose I want to attend an expensive concert. I know you would be unwilling to lend me the money if you knew (as is in fact the case) that I cannot repay you. So I tell you that I want to invest the money, and promise to repay you next week. By withholding crucial information, I prevent you from properly exercising your own powers of choice. I am thus treating you only as a means to my end. On Kant's view, I must give a rational person all the relevant information, and let them make up their own mind.

Kant's commitment to honouring value can be quite extreme, as in the following notorious example – familiar to anyone who has taken a first-year university ethics course.

Your friends are hiding in the cellar from the secret police. Although your friends are completely innocent, you know that the secret police will take them away and torture them to death. The secret police knock on your door and ask if you know where the fugitives are hiding. This is a routine inquiry, and you are a respectable citizen whose connection to the fugitives is unknown. If you lie, the secret police will believe you and go away. You must decide whether to lie to the secret police, or tell them the truth and allow your friends to be taken away and murdered. What should you do?

Kant says you must not lie, even in these circumstances. The secret police officers are rational autonomous agents, not machines or tools. Instead of using them as a means to your end (protecting your friends), you should respect them as ends-in-themselves. You should tell the secret police where your friends are, and then attempt to persuade them not to torture them. (Presumably you should do this without trying to persuade the secret police to lie to anyone else, such as their superiors.)

Most people find Kant's view crazy. Surely, given what you know about the intentions of the secret police, your obligation not to betray your friends should trump your general obligation not to tell lies. If you tell the truth, you are betraying your friends. This hardly seems to show much respect *for them*. Kant's response is that you are responsible for what *you do* (and for the immediate consequences of your actions), but you are not responsible for the decisions of other rational agents (or the consequences of those decisions). Part of the explanation for this lies in Kant's metaphysics – which is notoriously difficult to understand. Very briefly, Kant contrasts two ways you can think of a human being: as a physical object (subject to deterministic laws of causation and suitable for manipulation and use as a means like any other physical object), or as a free rational agent (whose decisions cannot be predicted and who should not be manipulated). If you lie to the secret police, you treat them as tools. You are then responsible for the outcome. (Suppose you lie to the secret police. They move immediately to the next house, and then happen to meet your friends on the road out of town. Because you treated the secret police as a means, you are now responsible for the fact that your friends are tortured.) On the other hand, to treat someone as a rational agent is to acknowledge that you cannot possibly predict their actions. So you do not know how they will respond to the truth. In particular, you cannot know in advance that a rational agent will fail to do the right thing. If you tell the truth, then you are not responsible for the outcome – no matter what the secret police choose to do.

Other elements of Kant's overall philosophical system take some of the sting out of his uncompromising moral views. In particular, the belief that human freedom transcends the deterministic world of cause and effect is one of three *postulates* of practical reason for Kant – three metaphysical claims that we must adopt if we are to make sense of our moral obligations. The other two postulates are the existence of God and the immortality of human beings. We have encountered Kant's postulates before, in our discussion of Sidgwick's dualism of practical reason in Chapter 2. While Kant's argument is highly controversial, its basic features are as follows. Theoretical speculation is based on our concepts, which are designed solely for the world we experience. Such speculation cannot take us beyond the world of experience. So it cannot tell us whether God exists, or whether we are immortal. However, morality tells me to aim for my own moral perfection and for a just world. These demands are incoherent and irrational unless there is an afterlife presided over by a benevolent deity. Belief in God is morally necessary. We have practical reasons to believe in God, and no theoretical reason not to. Therefore, belief in God is reasonable. If God is in the background ensuring that justice will prevail in the end, then it is reasonable for me to focus on my own duty, and leave the consequences to take care of themselves.

As we saw in Chapter 2, Sidgwick emphatically rejected Kant's solution to the dualism of practical reason. Our need to systematize ethics gives us an urgent reason to *hope* that the universe is user-friendly, and provides a very strong motivation to seek evidence of friendliness, but this is no reason to believe that the universe actually *is* friendly. Most contemporary utilitarians would follow Sidgwick here rather than Kant. We cannot bring in God to make ethics coherent. If we cannot be sure that God exists, then it is simply reckless to leave the consequences to take care of themselves.

Modern "Kantian ethicists" also depart from Kant when it comes to God and immortality – although they typically do follow Kant in his emphasis on freedom. The challenge for modern Kantians is to make Kant's views on lying plausible outside his strange metaphysical system. One place to begin is the fact that even Kant himself does not consistently adopt the extreme view that is often attributed to him. His moral writings as a whole present a more complex and nuanced position. Sometimes the appropriate way to respect humanity is to promote the welfare of others, or to enable them to pursue their own projects. Kant thus recognizes a duty of benevolence – one which can become quite demanding.

Like consequentialism, Kant's ethics is built on a strict commitment to impartiality. This clearly rules out any foundational role for partiality or concessions to the agent's self-interest. Kant includes positive duties to come to the aid of others. He distinguishes two types of duties: perfect and imperfect. The obligation not to lie is a perfect duty, unconditionally telling you exactly what to do. A perfect duty requires certain specific actions, and rules out others. By contrast, duties of benevolence are imperfect. There is no particular action you must perform to fulfil them. The duty to be benevolent requires you to perform *some* benevolent acts, but it does not tell you exactly which ones.

These imperfect duties threaten to prohibit any concern for your own happiness. While imperfect duties do not outweigh perfect duties, they presumably seek to fill up the space those duties leave open. Many patterns of behaviour are consistent with observance of all one's perfect duties. But if I am required to devote all my remaining energy to my imperfect duties, then Kantian ethics will be extremely demanding. Donating most of my income to charity does not look like a failure of self-respect, or a violation of any positive duty. (Unless, of course, I have made a very demanding promise. For instance, if I promise to give all my money to you, then I have a positive duty *not* to give it to charity. But this would hardly *reduce* the overall demands of morality.) The demands of Kantianism are thus very similar to those of consequentialism.

If we decide that a theory that only honours value is too austere, we might opt for a composite theory, where value is sometimes honoured and sometimes promoted. Perhaps some specific values (such as human freedom) are honoured, while others (such as human happiness) are promoted. The challenge would then be to balance the two components. It is possible that this combined view might solve the injustice objection by finding a middle road between consequentialism (which permits too much lying or killing) and pure Kantianism (which permits none). But, if consequentialism and pure Kantianism are both too demanding, it is hard to see how a theory combining the two could be any less demanding.

Other responses to value

In recent years, some moral philosophers have explored a number of other responses to value. Two examples are *expression* and *admiration*. Suppose you believe that athletic achievement is valuable. Instead of *promoting* athletic achievement (by donating large sums of money to your university's athletic programme), or *honouring* athletic achievement (by kissing the feet of successful athletes), you might decide to *embody* or *express* the value of athletic achievement by becoming a successful athlete yourself. Similarly, you might respond to the value of knowledge by gaining as much knowledge as possible. Or suppose a certain type of beauty is valuable. You respond not by producing beauty, nor by respecting beauty, nor by becoming beautiful, but by *admiring* (or perhaps even worshipping) the beauty you find around you. Some values call for *appreciation* rather than *action*.

As we saw in our discussion of indirect utilitarianism and rule-utilitarianism in Chapter 6, consequentialists can incorporate all these alternative responses as indirect strategies to promote value. A non-consequentialist response to one value may even promote a different value. Worshipping beauty and respecting athleticism might be the best ways to maximize happiness. Consequentialists argue that, in a full moral theory, we must know how to balance different responses against one another. How do we decide whether to promote value x, or honour value y, or express value z? Indirect consequentialism or rule-consequentialism provide simple ways to balance these responses, at least in theory. For instance, a rule-consequentialist can say we should imitate the pattern of responses to value which, if adopted by everyone, would produce the best consequences. This would lead to a consequentialist account of virtue – where virtues are those character traits that produce the most beneficial outcomes. Non-consequentialists regard this indirect recognition as insufficient. Honouring, expressing and admiring are intrinsically appropriate responses to value whose full moral significance cannot be captured by consequentialist paraphrases.

Are utilitarians committed to consequentialism?

In contemporary moral philosophy, utilitarianism is presented as a version of consequentialism. Utilitarianism *is* consequentialism (morality promotes value) *plus* welfarism (value is aggregate human welfare). But this has not always been true. Some early utilitarians (such as William Godwin) clearly were consequentialists. But the situation is much less clear with others. The defining feature of utilitarianism is the idea that morality is concerned with human welfare. It does not necessarily follow that utilitarians are committed to the impersonal promotion of aggregate welfare. Recall (from Chapter 5) Rawls' objection that utilitarianism ignores the separateness of persons. This complaint would have puzzled J. S. Mill, with his emphasis on the values of individuality and liberty, and his goal of protecting the individual from the tyranny of the majority. Mill's view often seems to be that the role of moral codes and social institutions is to ensure that *each person* enjoys a worthwhile life, with adequate personal liberty, input into political decision-making, and material comfort. It is thus unfair to criticize Mill (or Bentham) for not proving *consequentialism* (or for not demolishing modern objections to consequentialism), as this was never their intention.

Suppose we define *non-maximizing utilitarianism* as the view that the right action (or the correct code of rules, or the correct set of institutions) is one that promotes human happiness for each individual, without seeking to maximize total well-being. Non-maximizing utilitarianism seems to avoid both the injustice and demandingness objections. Unfortunate individuals will no longer have their basic rights and interests sacrificed to provide small benefits to many others, and no one is required to sacrifice her own basic needs to benefit others. However, things are not so simple. What if we cannot provide a worthwhile life for everyone? What if we must choose between injustices? Even if we no longer have to kill one person to save many others from inconvenience (as in the football game tale), we may still have to kill one to prevent a riot where many would be killed (as in the sheriff tale). So long as some people's basic needs go unmet, this new theory also threatens to place extreme demands on those whose basic needs are comparatively secure. We need more guidance on how to balance conflicting needs or interests. Non-maximizing utilitarianism does not tell us how to resolve all the complex conflicts uncovered by our tales. But perhaps it does provide a guiding principle for social reform – one that does respect the separateness of persons. Non-maximizing utilitarianism might thus be a fruitful way forward for those modern utilitarians who want to avoid the puzzles and demands of modern consequentialism. Another advantage is that, because it rejects aggregation and maximization, non-maximizing utilitarianism may be easier to apply to the real world than traditional maximizing consequentialism. As we shall now see, this may be a very significant advantage.

Key points

- Consequentialism says the right action is the one that produces the most value – whatever definition of value we use.

- Utilitarians can be either consequentialist or non-consequentialist.
- Consequentialists can be either utilitarian or non-utilitarian.
- Satisficing consequentialism says we are only obliged to produce a good enough outcome.
- Hybrid views supplement consequentialism with agent-centred prerogatives, allowing us to give disproportionate weight to our own interests.
- Both satisficing consequentialism and hybrid views have difficulty accommodating the distinction between doing and allowing.
- Kantian ethicists focus on honouring value (especially the value of rational agents), rather than promoting value.

eight

Practicality

One enduring criticism of utilitarianism has always been that, as it rests upon precise calculations of utility, it is unworkable. This chapter explores this objection, with a focus on the following questions. How does utilitarianism deal with uncertainty? Can utility be measured? Does utilitarianism presuppose that utility can be measured? If utility cannot be precisely measured, what guidance can utilitarianism offer? The practical objection to utilitarianism is straightforward.

1. Utilitarianism tells us to maximize human happiness.
2. Therefore, if we do not know what would maximize human happiness, then we cannot know what utilitarianism tells us to do.
3. But we have no idea how to maximize human happiness.
4. Therefore, we have no idea what utilitarianism tells us to do.

We explore various utilitarian responses to this objection, and its impact on the shape of utilitarianism. Two kinds of uncertainty plague utilitarianism, as we do not know what *will* happen (practical uncertainty), and we do not know how to *evaluate* what will happen (uncertainty about values). We begin with practical uncertainty.

Actualism versus probabilism

This simple tale illustrates a common objection to utilitarianism. Utilitarianism says you should have pressed button Y, as this would have saved Bertold and thereby produced the best outcome. But you could not possibly have known this in advance, as the machine is completely random. Indeed, *no one* could have known what you should do. Utilitarianism is thus both unfair and totally useless. This problem arises constantly in real life, as we never know all the consequences in advance.

The most common utilitarian response is to distinguish between *actual results* and *probable results*. *Actualist* utilitarianism says you acted wrongly, as things would have turned out better if you had pressed the other button. By contrast, *probabilist* utilitarianism says that you acted rightly, as pressing button X was far more likely to lead to good results than pressing button Y. Most utilitarians base their judgements of right and wrong on probabilities not actual results. Unfortunately, this leads to many new difficulties. Actualist utilitarians evaluate actions simply by comparing the values of the resulting outcomes. Probabilistic utilitarians face a more complex task, as they must consider both the value of each outcome and its probability. There are many different ways to evaluate actions using both values and probabilities. Here are the three simplest.

1. *Maximin.* The value of an action is the value of the worst outcome it might produce. If I stay at home, the worst possible result is boredom. If I go out, the worst possible result is death in a traffic accident. Staying at home is the better option.
2. *Expected value.* We multiply the value of each possible outcome by its probability, and then add the results together. The simplest

way to illustrate this idea is with money. Suppose option A offers a 50 per cent chance of £100 and a 50 per cent chance of £200, while option B offers a 99 per cent chance of £0 and a 1 per cent chance of £1,000,000. The expected value of option A is $(0.5 \times 100) + (0.5 \times 200) = 150$. The expected value of option B is $(0.99 \times 0) + (0.01 \times 1,000,000) = 10,000$. So B is the better option.

3. *Maximax.* The value of an action is the value of the best outcome it might produce. If I watch television, the best possible result is mild amusement. If I gamble all my savings and all my available credit on the internet, the best possible result is that I win a fortune. High-stakes gambling is the better option. (I should also answer all anonymous emails offering me £50,000,000 in exchange for my bank account details – because they might be genuine.)

Maximin and maximax are both dubious. If I follow these strategies, I will either take so few risks that I do not live at all, or so many risks that my life will almost certainly be destroyed. Most utilitarians prefer expected value. The right action is the one with the highest expected value. In our earlier example, the expected value method may seem to give the wrong answer. Imagine you have absolutely no money except what you will receive from the option you choose. In real life, most people would take option A (which guarantees you at least £100) rather than option B (which will almost certainly leave you with nothing). If the expected value method tells you to opt for B, does that not prove it is a bad decision procedure?

Utilitarians will reply that, although we *illustrated* the expected value method using money, we should *apply* it using well-being rather than money. Most people experience *diminishing marginal returns* from money. If you start with nothing, then the first £100 will produce a great improvement in your well-being; whereas an increase of £100 might have almost no impact on the well-being of someone who already has £1,000,000. To provide an artificially exact numerical example, suppose you assign the following well-being values to the various possible outcomes.

£	Well-being
0	0
100	10
200	15
1,000,000	25

If you calculate the expected value of the two options using these well-being values, you get a very different result. The expected value of option A is $(10 \times 0.5) + (15 \times 0.5) = 12.5$, while the expected value of option B is $(0 \times 0.99) + (25 \times 0.01) = 0.25$. So A is much the better option.

But now consider a different lottery, with the same well-being values associated with each sum of money. Option C offers a 70 per cent chance of £200 and a 30 per cent chance of £0, while option D offers a 100 per cent chance of £100. In terms of well-being, the expected value of option C is $(0.7 \times 15) + (0.3 \times 0) = 10.5$. The expected value of option D is $(1.00 \times 10) = 10$. So, according to the expected value method, C is the better option. Some people would still prefer D, as it guarantees that you will get a well-being of 10, whereas C does not. If this is your reaction, then you might want a more *risk-averse* decision procedure than the expected value method – perhaps some complicated formula combining elements of both expected value and maximin.

Objective versus subjective probabilities

> **Two buttons II**
> The evil genius tricks you. Button X gives Bertold a 1 per cent chance of sur-vival and button Y a 99 per cent chance. But you falsely believe that button X gives Bertold a 99 per cent chance of survival and button Y only a 1 per cent chance. So you press button X. The machine selects a number other than 100, and Bertold is electrocuted. Have you done the wrong thing?

Once we have decided how we will use probabilities, we must next decide *which* probabilities. This new tale illustrates a new objection that now arises. Button Y gave the higher probability of success. So util-itarianism says you should push button Y. But you could not possibly have known this in advance, as the evil genius is your only source of information. So utilitarianism is still unfair and useless. In reply, utilitarians distinguish between *objective* and *subjective* probabilities. *Objective* utilitarianism says you did wrong, as Y was in fact 99 per cent likely to lead to electrocution. On the other hand, *subjective* utilitarian-ism says you did right, because Y had the lower probability of harm *so far as you knew*. Some utilitarians rely entirely on subjective probabil-ities. After all, what could be the relevance of probabilities you know nothing about? Others use both objective and subjective probabilities for different purposes. For instance, some utilitarians use objective probabilities to identify the *rightness* of an action, but they use subjective probabilities to *praise and blame* people. The right action gives the highest objective probability of human happiness. But you should not be blamed if you chose the action you *believed* gave the highest objective probability of human happiness. If you try to do the right thing, then you should be praised, not blamed – even if, due to your ignorance of probabilities, you fail to do the right thing.

Two buttons III
You are in the room with two buttons. There is an instruction manual on the desk. You have not read the instruction manual. So you have no idea which button to push. You reason as follows. "Given my ignorance, each button has a 50 per cent chance of being the right one. Therefore, the subjective probability of getting the right result is the same for each option, and they yield the same subjective expected human happiness. So it does not matter which option I choose." Have you done the wrong thing?

This tale illustrates an intriguing issue raised by the distinction between subjective and objective probabilities: *culpable ignorance*. Your behaviour in this tale is clearly wrong. If you select a button at random without bothering to read the instruction manual, then clearly you should be blamed for recklessly endangering your friend in the electric chair. Does this mean you should not rely on subjective probabilities at all?

A utilitarian will reply that you have misdescribed your situation. You are thinking that you have two options: push button X or push button Y. But this is too simple. You obviously have a third option: read the instruction manual and *then* choose which button to push. Because you are unaware of the workings of the machine, you know that reading the instruction manual will improve your chances of doing the right thing. So this new option offers better subjective probabilities than any alternative. So you should be blamed. (By contrast, if you were sure the book was not an instruction manual, then you would not be blamed for not reading it.)

Intrapersonal comparisons

Suppose we accept that utilitarians can avoid many objections by shifting their focus from actual results to subjective probabilities. We turn now to a series of objections to utilitarianism that focus on the measurement of human well-being. These objections arise even if we know exactly what results each possible action would produce. We begin with the simplest case, where your actions impact on only one other person. If utilitarianism cannot cope in this case, then it cannot hope to be a plausible theory.

The isolation chamber
Jane suffers from a deficiency of the immune system requiring her to live in an isolation chamber. You are her only link to the outside world. Your decision has no impact on your own well-being. As a utilitarian, you aim to base your decision solely on Jane's well-being. What should you do?

Sometimes the impact on Jane's well-being is comparatively easy to estimate. You should refrain from giving her electric shocks, feeding her cyanide capsules or attacking her with a machete. As a philosopher familiar with bizarre science fiction thought experiments, you know it is *conceivable* that Jane has such a strange metabolism that electric shocks give her pleasure, cyanide is good for her digestion, or a machete attack would cause her limbs to grow back healthier and stronger. However, you know enough about human beings in general to know that electrocution, cyanide or amputation almost certainly will not enhance Jane's well-being or health. As your utilitarianism uses subjective probabilities rather than actual results, you can disregard these bizarre possibilities.

Other cases are more difficult. Suppose you have a kilogram of chocolate and a kilogram of strawberries. The robot used to transfer items into the isolation chamber is very delicate, and can only deliver one kilogram of food each day. You must decide whether to give Jane the chocolate or the strawberries. Or suppose Jane has successfully applied to two long-distance vocational courses, but there is only time for her to study one of them. You must decide whether to give her a career as a philosopher or as a dentist.

General information about human beings does not seem so useful here. Suppose you discover that 60 per cent of people prefer chocolate, while 40 per cent prefer strawberries; and that 70 per cent of people prefer dentistry to philosophy, while 30 per cent prefer philosophy to dentistry. This does not give you enough information. (Suppose you were deciding, not just for Jane, but for everyone in the world. Would you give everyone chocolate and make them all dentists? This hardly seems the right result.)

The best utilitarian response is this. If you cannot obtain *any* individual information about Jane, then you *should* use general statistical information and give her chocolate and dentistry. (This has the added bonus that, when the chocolate destroys her teeth, she will be able to fix them.) How else could you possibly decide? On the other hand, your knowledge of human nature tells you that information about Jane would greatly enhance your chances of making the right decision for her. So you should strive to acquire such information. You might study Jane's physiology (to predict the impact of chocolate or strawberries on her general health or pleasure), or administer various questionnaires, or study the consumption and career choices of Jane's relations (to see if she has a genetic predisposition towards strawberries or philosophy). Even if no such information is available, you can still avoid reliance on general statistical information. This is because one source of information is always available to you. You could offer Jane herself a *choice* between chocolate and strawberries, or between philosophy and dentistry, and let her have what she chooses. If she chooses chocolate over strawberries, then chocolate enhances her well-being more than strawberries.

It is obvious that a utilitarian who adopts a preference-based theory of well-being will want to give Jane what she wants. However, the great beauty of this strategy is that it works whatever your theory of well-being. Hedonists are not directly interested in Jane's preferences or choices. They want to maximize Jane's pleasure. However, if Jane is better placed than you to judge what will give her pleasure, then the fact that she prefers strawberries is the best evidence you could have that strawberries are better for her. As you might expect, things are potentially more complicated for objective list theorists. Even if choice is on our list, other list-items may be better served by an option Jane does not prefer. In theory, it is possible that dentistry constitutes a more genuinely worthwhile achievement than philosophy, and that this advantage outweighs Jane's own preferences. If Jane prefers philosophy, then she may simply be mistaken. However, as we saw in Chapter 4, any plausible objective list theory is extremely unlikely to override Jane's choices. Most lists give significance to both pleasure and preference. So the objective list theory will usually coincide with hedonism and preference theory, especially when the latter two theories agree. If Jane prefers chocolate and gets more pleasure from it, then it is almost certainly better for her. Furthermore, most modern list theorists give special weight to autonomy and choice. Some go so far as to say that a life cannot be valuable unless the person chooses it. On this view, even if dentistry was generally much better than philosophy, chosen-philosophy must trump forced-dentistry.

So far we have pictured utilitarians as trying to maximize well-being understood in terms of a definite theory. In practice, most contemporary utilitarians are unsure exactly which account of well-being is correct. By allowing people to make their own decisions we can maximize human welfare, even though we are not sure what human welfare *is*.

So much for the simplest case. Further difficulties arise when more than one person is involved. Most of the common objections to utilitarianism arise when we can only provide a benefit for one person by imposing a cost on others (either third parties or ourselves). Indeed, problems arise even when no costs are involved, and we must decide whom to benefit.

Two isolation chambers

You have two patients in separate isolation chambers – Jane and Jerry. You have a kilogram of chocolate and a kilogram of strawberries. For some technical reason that is too boring to explain here, you must give all the chocolate to one person and all the strawberries to the other. What should you do?

Your choice would be easy if one patient preferred chocolate while the other preferred strawberries, or chocolate were particularly bad for one patient. Unfortunately, they both prefer chocolate to strawberries – and neither patient has a chocolate allergy or a cholesterol problem. You also have one dentistry scholarship and one philosophy scholarship. Both Jane and Jerry prefer dentistry to philosophy. As a utilitarian, you want to maximize human welfare. So you must ask: who will get *more* welfare from receiving chocolate rather than strawberries? Who will benefit *more* from the opportunity to become a dentist rather than a philosopher?

You need more information. You know who prefers what. You must now discover the comparative strengths of their preferences. You must make an *inter*personal comparison. It is not enough to know that Jane is better-off with chocolate rather than strawberries. You must know *how much* better-off. You must compare the outcome where Jane gets chocolate and Jerry gets strawberries with the outcome where Jerry gets the chocolate and Jane the strawberries. One obvious problem is that you cannot tell, by observing people's choices, whether they regard a particular choice as very important or completely trivial. Perhaps Jane would be almost as happy with philosophy as with dentistry, whereas Jerry will be heartbroken unless he fulfils his boyhood dental dream.

We might begin with two *intra*personal comparisons. Suppose you ask each of your patients the following question. "If you were able to choose either what you will eat or your career (but not both), which would you choose?" This will tell us whether eating chocolate (as opposed to strawberries) is more important to Jane than becoming a dentist (rather than a philosopher). This test may help, as different people value different things. Perhaps food is more important to Jane, while Jerry cares more about career choice. But suppose both patients care more about what they eat than what they study. Both prefer chocolate-and-philosophy over strawberries-and-dentistry. You need more detailed information. You need to know how much more important each decision is to each person.

Another solution is to measure different people's preferences in a common currency. Suppose you give Jane and Jerry £100 each. You then ask them how much money they would spend to buy the right to decide who eats what, and how much they would spend to decide their career. Suppose Jane allocates £67 to food choice and £33 to career choice, while Jerry allocates £80 to food and £20 to career. You might conclude that the food choice is four times as important for Jerry, but only twice as important to Jane. So Jerry should make the food choice and Jane the career choice.

This solution assumes that one person's total preference strength is the same as another person's. But this might not be true. Suppose Jane has very strong preferences about *everything*, while *all* Jerry's preferences are weak. Well-being is maximized if Jane makes every single decision. (This seems a bit unfair on Jerry, but at least he will not mind too much.) You might think this problem only arises on a preference-based account of well-being. But we should note that the same problem can also arise on a hedonist view. Everyday activities might give Jane great pleasures and pains, but leave Jerry comparatively unaffected.

How can we know whether Jane has stronger preferences than Jerry? We cannot look at how she allocates her money, because giving both people the same money assumes their total preference strength is equal. One common solution is to allocate goods on the basis of effort. Suppose you use a competitive examination to determine careers. The person with the stronger preference will work harder, so well-being is maximized if that person gets the dental career. If Jane has much stronger preferences about everything, then she will work harder and do better. We can then allocate other goods by attaching a higher income to the more desirable career. Because Jane has worked harder, she deserves a dentist's wealth. Her money then buys all the other things she wants.

Even this strategy is not foolproof. We said earlier that Jane has very strong preferences about *everything*. Suppose both Jane and Jerry prefer television to studying. Jane's preference for television is very strong. Jerry's preference for dentistry over philosophy is weak, but his preference for television over study is even weaker. Jerry works harder – not because he cares more about dentistry, but because he does not much mind studying. So the exam system will not maximize welfare.

This brings us to another objection to utilitarianism. In this case – where Jane really does have strong preferences about everything – well-being would be maximized if Jane watched television while Jerry studied, and Jerry then sat the exam on Jane's behalf, enabling *her* to become a dentist. This seems very unfair on Jerry, suggesting that welfare maximization is not a desirable goal. How should utilitarians react?

An alternative for the utilitarian – in the spirit of the classical utilitarian rejection of radical scepticism – would be simply to say that extreme sceptical possibilities (How can we be sure that A's preferences are not *all* twice as strong as B's? How can we be sure that A does not get twice as much pleasure *from everything* as B?) are not worth bothering about in practice. Perhaps utilitarians have no guarantee against such scepticism, but who does? Another alternative is to regard the assumption of equal total preference strength as a *moral commitment*, not an empirical claim. We give each person £100, not because we believe that their preferences are equally strong, but because we regard their lives as equally important. We aim at the fairest and best distribution of welfare, not at maximum total human well-being.

This may look like a departure from utilitarianism. If we define utilitarianism in terms of the maximization of aggregate well-being, then this is perhaps correct. However, we could adopt a broader definition, linking utilitarianism to the promotion of well-being without requiring maximization or aggregation. We saw one example in the previous chapter, when we discussed non-maximizing utilitarianism. This view would combine very well with our present suggestion that, especially when choosing public policies, utilitarians should give each person equal weight. This is certainly in conformity with the dictum that Mill attributes to Bentham as expressing the essence of the utilitarian tradition: "Each to count for one, and none for more than one."

Opponents might question whether non-maximizing utilitarianism really can avoid the commitments of maximizing utilitarianism. For instance, even under non-maximizing utilitarianism we are often required to allocate goods between competing agents. So we still need robust interpersonal comparisons of well-being.

Utilitarianism requires a further dimension of interpersonal comparison, arising from the fact that most utilitarians focus on probabilities rather than actual results. We can illustrate this new dimension using another new tale.

Two isolation chambers II

You have chocolate to give Jane or Jerry, who both like chocolate. As Jane likes chocolate more than Jerry does, you want to give it to her. Unfortunately, the robot servicing Jane's isolation chamber is much less reliable than Jerry's robot. There is a 50 per cent chance that Jane's robot will explode, destroying the chocolate. So you must choose between a 50 per cent chance of chocolate for Jane and a 100 per cent chance of chocolate for Jerry. What should you do?

Suppose eating chocolate raises Jane's well-being by x, while it raises Jerry's well-being by y (where $x > y$). If you try to send the chocolate to Jane, the expected value is $x/2$. If you send it to Jerry, the expected value is y. If you aim to maximize total expected well-being, then you now need to know whether $x/2$ is greater than y. Does Jane get more than twice as much well-being from the chocolate as Jerry? If she does, then you should take the risk. If not, then you should play safe and give the chocolate to Jerry.

In technical terms, you need a *cardinal* scale of well-being, not just an *ordinal* scale. To illustrate these notions, suppose you are measuring the weight of objects. You might begin with a very simple set of scales, where you place two objects on different sides and observe which one falls to the ground. This measurement device provides an *ordinal* scale. If you have time, you can compare each pair of objects and place them in order from the heaviest to the lightest. However, this is the only information you will gather. You cannot compare differences between objects. You have ordinal information but not cardinal information. By contrast, if you have a modern set of bathroom scales, then you can directly measure the weight of each object. This enables you to compare the differences between weights.

It is worth nothing that the same problem can arise even for a single individual. Suppose you are using the robot to transport your own food. Because chocolate interferes with the robot's circuitry, you must choose between a 50 per cent chance of chocolate and a 100 per cent chance of strawberries. Is chocolate twice as important as strawberries? In the one-person case, we might answer this question simply by offering you a choice between a 50 per cent chance of chocolate and 100 per cent chance of strawberries. If you take the gamble, then chocolate is at least twice as valuable to you as strawberries; otherwise it is not. If we have to compare different people's preferences, then perhaps we can extend this solution to the case of many people.

Even a cardinal scale may not give us all the information we need. We can introduce one remaining problem by contrasting the measurement of weight with the measurement of temperature. Both the Fahrenheit and Celsius scales provide cardinal information. Both scales can tell you, not only that Florida is warmer than Canada, but also that the difference in temperature between Florida and Canada is greater than the difference between England and Scotland. However, neither the Fahrenheit scale nor the Celsius scale can tell you whether Florida is *twice as hot* as Canada. This is because, on both scales, the zero point is chosen arbitrarily. (For instance, 20 degrees Celsius looks twice as hot as 10 degrees Celsius. But if we convert those exact temperatures to Fahrenheit, we get 50 and 68, and the latter no longer looks twice as hot.) Your bathroom scales, by contrast, do provide this extra information because, unlike the temperatures scales, their zero point is not arbitrary. You can say that your cat is twice as heavy as your dog. The following tale suggests that we also need a non-arbitrary zero level when we are dealing with human well-being.

Two isolation chambers III

Jane and Jerry are trapped in their isolation chambers. Due to a power failure, both are running out of oxygen. You only have one robot strong enough to save a human being. There is no time to save both people. Jane is happier than Jerry. She will enjoy more happiness per year then Jerry. However, the tracks to Jane's isolation chamber are damaged. There is a 50 per cent chance the robot will malfunction en route, and both people will die. You must choose between a 50 per cent chance of saving Jane and the certainty of saving Jerry. So you must find out whether Jane would enjoy at least twice as much happiness (over the rest of her life) as Jerry. How might you get this information?

Can utilitarianism cope in the real world?

So far in this chapter – and throughout most of this book – we have applied act-utilitarianism to very simple tales. This is because our focus has been on theoretical issues, and we have been concerned to prove, at least, that the measurements required by utilitarianism are not theoretically impossible. However, many modern utilitarians apply the utilitarian test not just to isolated acts or individual decision-procedures, but to the evaluation of whole codes of rules, or the social institutions of an entire society. Opponents argue that, in the complex modern world, uncertainty must paralyse utilitarianism. There are two reasons for this.

1. *We cannot get information about everyone's well-being.* No one can obtain reliable information about the well-being of very large numbers of people, as we cannot undertake detailed studies of individual preferences, or construct elaborate artificial auctions across whole populations. Even if we knew exactly what would happen if we enacted a code of rules, we cannot hope to measure aggregate well-being.
2. *We cannot predict the impact of individual actions – let alone complete codes of rules.* This objection applies especially to rule-utilitarianism or institutional utilitarianism. Even a perfect measure of well-being would be useless, as we do not know what would happen if everyone followed one set of rules rather than another. The impact of adopting new moral rules or institutions across a whole society cannot possibly be calculated.

Utilitarians have two main replies to this pair of objections: they can search for proxies for welfare, or defend a more moderate theory such as piecemeal utilitarianism or conservative utilitarianism. We begin with the first option. We often can know that one outcome is better than another even when we cannot precisely measure well-being. We do this by measuring *proxies* for well-being: information typically correlated with key components of well-being. If a policy would increase average levels of health, income, literacy, civil rights and political freedoms, then this is very good evidence that it will improve human well-being, even if we cannot precisely calculate the total gain in aggregate well-being. Much of contemporary welfare economics and development economics can be seen as the search for reliable proxies that are *both* closely connected to important elements of human well-being *and* comparatively easy to measure.

The second route is to adopt a more modest approach to utilitarian calculations. Rule-utilitarianism seems implausible if it requires us to find a complete ideal code of rules. Some rule-utilitarians deny that it does require this. Rule-utilitarianism need not be wholesale and radical. It can be piecemeal and conservative. Even if we cannot determine the ideal code of rules in every detail, we can still know that it will include rule *x* and not rule *y*. We may know that any code including a robust prohibition on torture will produce better consequences than a code lacking this prohibition. So we know that torture is wrong, even if our knowledge of other moral matters is incomplete. Or you might calculate that the ideal code will include certain basic freedoms, even though you cannot be certain where those freedoms will lead. Most defences of rule-utilitarianism (and of indirect utilitarianism) are piecemeal in this way.

Conservatives often object that, instead of embarking on utilitarian reform, we should use tried and tested codes of moral rules. Many utilitarians embrace this objection. If a code of rules has enabled our society to survive and flourish, then this is good evidence that those rules promote human well-being. This establishes a *prima facie* case in favour of existing rules. So we should only adopt a new rule if we are reasonably sure it will do better. Departures are most likely to be justified if we can show either that an existing rule only promoted well-being due to specific circumstances which have now changed, or if we can find some explanation why a particular rule has persisted despite being detrimental to human well-being. For instance, we might uncover a conspiracy among powerful individuals who benefit from the rule – as Bentham claimed in his critiques of the legal profession of his day. If we find evidence that the status quo has a disreputable origin, this may encourage us to examine possible alternatives. We would then reject the status quo, not because of its origins *per se*, but because some specific alternative promises better results.

Utilitarians could also draw on the emerging discipline of *positive psychology* – the empirical study of happiness. Measuring happiness by the simple method of administering questionnaires asking people how happy they are, researchers have found correlations between happiness and other factors that are remarkably stable across different populations – even across different countries. These range from the comparatively obvious (people are happier if they are healthier and have stable personal relationships) to the controversial (people are happier in societies where taxation is used to make incomes more equal; beyond a comparatively low level, money does not make people happier). While philosophers might question the assumption that these questionnaires really measure well-being, the results provide a practical utilitarian with many useful public policy suggestions.

Liberty, equality, and democracy

To illustrate how utilitarians might cope with the bewildering complexity of the modern world, we finish by considering the utilitarian attitude to three key contemporary moral ideals: liberty, equality and democracy. As we saw in Chapter 2, J. S. Mill combined utilitarianism with a strong commitment to both liberty and social equality. Our discussions in this chapter reinforce Mill's utilitarian defence of liberty. Whatever the details of our theory of well-being, things will generally go best overall if people are free to decide for themselves how they will live – from comparatively trivial questions such as choosing a meal to life-defining questions of career or sexual lifestyle. If we are rule-utilitarians, then we should expect the ideal code of rules to leave most important decisions to the individual. (This is especially true under non-maximizing utilitarianism. If our aim is to give *each person* a good life, then we will hardly ever be justified in restricting personal freedoms.)

However, for the utilitarian, freedom is primarily of *instrumental* value. The value of freedom may be very great, but it is not absolute. Utilitarians have always emphasized that freedom can have detrimental effects, especially at a societal or global level. Mill himself is a good example. Mill is often presented today as a defender of free market capitalism – and he certainly did believe the utilitarian society would leave most issues of production and consumption to the market. However, Mill was also aware of the risk that unfettered capitalism would lead to a great concentration of wealth in the hands of a few people. For a utilitarian, this inequality is not intrinsically bad. The problem is that, if people's power is unequal, then we cannot be confident that freedom of choice maximizes well-being. As we saw in our simple examples earlier in this chapter, an idealized auction only promotes well-being if everyone has the same amount of money to bid. If I have £100 and Bill has £1,000,000,000, then Bill's slightest whim will swamp my strongest desire.

So the utilitarian (instrumental) commitment to liberty is tempered by an (instrumental) commitment to equality. The utilitarian ideal is a world where, beginning from a position of equality, everyone makes their own choices. Conflicts between liberty and equality abound in public policy. While utilitarianism does not provide a simple answer to these conflicts, it does provide a helpful way to think about them. Instead of treating liberty and equality as absolute ideals that cannot be compromised or traded off against one another, utilitarianism asks us to measure them against each other – and against any other ideals we might have – using the common metric of human well-being.

The utilitarian arguments for liberty and equality come together in the strong utilitarian support for democracy – which utilitarians see as a system of government where each person (equally) has the liberty to decide how he or she will be governed. As we saw in Chapter 2, the utilitarian argument for democracy goes back at least to J. S. Mill. The Nobel Prize winning economist Amartya Sen has recently provided a striking illustration of the claim that democracy is the most reliable way to promote people's interests, by arguing that only democracy can reliably prevent famine.

> It is not surprising that no famine has taken place in the history of the world in a functioning democracy, be it economically rich (as in contemporary Western Europe or North America) or relatively poor (as in postindependence India, or Botswana, or Zimbabwe). Famines have tended to occur in colonial territories governed by rulers from elsewhere (as in British India or in an Ireland administered by alienated English rulers), or in one-party states (as in the Ukraine in the 1930s, or China during 1958–1961, or Cambodia in the 1970s), or in military dictatorships (as in Ethiopia, or Somalia, or some of the Sahel countries in the near past).
>
> (Sen, *Development as Freedom*, 16)

It is a sad irony that Sen lists Zimbabwe as a poor famine-free democracy. Zimbabwe's current transition from democracy to one-party state – and the accompanying food crisis – reinforces Sen's conclusions. Sen's explanation is that the combination of a free press and democracy provides rulers with strong incentives to prevent famine. Despotic rulers have no such incentive, so they permit famine. Famine is bad for people, on any remotely plausible theory of well-being. If democracy is the only system of government that reliably avoids famine, then this is a very strong *prima facie* argument for democracy. Other recent studies have established positive correlations between democracy and a variety of indicators of well-being (including real net income per head, economic growth, infant survival rates and life expectancy at birth). Partha Dasgupta concludes a recent summary of that literature with the following observation.

> The argument that democracy is a luxury that poor countries cannot afford is buried by the data, such as they are.
>
> (Dasgupta, *Human Well-being and the Natural Environment*, 75)

Of course, this simple utilitarian argument does not tell us what form of democracy is best. Utilitarians need much more information before choosing one particular democratic system. For instance, one question of contemporary interest is whether utilitarians should support a purely majoritarian system of parliamentary sovereignty (as found in the UK) or a system where the legislature is constrained by an entrenched constitution interpreted by unelected judges (as in the USA). Here, the empirical evidence is much harder to assess.

Utilitarianism cannot provide all the answers. However, its defenders argue that this is because it recognizes that political decisions depend, in part, on extremely complex empirical questions. Measurement problems arise from the nature of the world, not from any defect in utilitarianism.

Key points

- Most utilitarians focus on the expected value of actions, not on actual results.
- Utilitarians can use either objective or subjective probabilities. (Some use objective probabilities for wrongness, and subjective probabilities to assign blame.)
- Utilitarians need both intrapersonal and interpersonal comparisons of well-being.
- Utilitarianism can offer useful advice in the real world, even if we cannot make exact calculations of well-being.

nine

The future of utilitarianism

Utilitarianism tells us, not only what to think about particular issues, but also which issues to think about. In particular, utilitarianism tells us that the most important moral issues are those where the greatest amount of human happiness (or human misery) is at stake. While the happiness of presently existing people in our own society is certainly significant, its value is dwarfed by the welfare of the billions of people who already exist in other lands, and of all the people who might exist in the future. For the utilitarian, the most important moral issues are those relating to these two groups of people. Utilitarianism has always been, and continues to be, most interesting and most relevant when applied to changing social circumstances, or to issues that have been under-appreciated by other moral theories. The focus of this chapter is on outlining the questions raised by utilitarianism, rather than on any detailed exploration of particular answers.

A global ethic

Utilitarianism arose in Britain in the eighteenth and nineteenth centuries in a society of very limited democracy, widespread poverty and considerable corruption and inefficiency. The critiques and activities of utilitarians played a key role in improving this situation. In utilitarian terms, modern Western societies are much better today than in the days of the early utilitarians. But our global situation is, in many crucial respects, at least as bad. The world of international affairs is not democratic, and the gap between the world's richest and poorest nations (in terms of wealth, life expectancy, literacy, civil and political rights, or health) is far greater than the gap between rich and poor in even the most unequal individual country. Contemporary utilitarians draw on earlier utilitarianism to provide critiques of international law and politics that are often very radical.

For utilitarians, the foundation of all morality – both individual and global – is the equal importance of the well-being of each human individual. Utilitarianism bases morality, not just on the welfare of New Zealanders or Americans or Europeans, but of all people in the world. Conventional global ethics gives significant weight to national boundaries. Most of us intuitively think that our obligations to people in our own country are much greater than our obligations to people in distant nations. Natural resources such as oil or good soil are thought to be owned by nations, rather than by the global community as a whole. In conventional global ethics, and especially in international law, the concept of nationhood is *foundational*. Utilitarians reject this approach. Utilitarianism is a global ethic, where all distinctions between people must be justified in utilitarian terms. If we want to attach importance to nations, we must justify this decision by showing how it promotes global well-being.

In this book, we have seen several times that, within any particular society, utilitarians favour democracy, liberty and equality. One good starting point for any utilitarian global ethic is to apply these ideals at a global level. What would a democratic, liberal, egalitarian international order look like? Would it be better than the global status quo?

As we saw in Chapters 2 and 8, utilitarians favour democracy for many reasons. Most of these carry over to the international arena. Individual participation in global decision-making is needed if global decisions are to reflect the values of all individuals, and to promote everyone's well-being. Indeed, *this* argument for democracy is perhaps even stronger in the global case, as decision-makers are even less likely to have the motivation and information necessary to take appropriate account of the interests of people in other nations. It is hardly surprising that international institutions, rules or policies do not adequately take account of the interests of the world's most vulnerable people, even when all those involved make an honest attempt to promote those interests.

On the other hand, some utilitarian arguments suggest limits on global democracy. Participation in decision-making within a group containing the six billion inhabitants of our planet is unlikely to provide each of us with a real sense of participation in "my community". Drawing on one of Mill's arguments, we might argue that, if individuals are to be meaningfully autonomous, then they should be able to contribute to those decisions which most affect them. So any global utilitarian parliament would grant considerable autonomy to local groups.

It is, of course, impossible to predict in any detail what a democratic world order might look like. But, as we saw in Chapter 8, this does not mean utilitarianism is useless. We might begin by imagining a very simple model of a global democracy. Suppose we elect a global parliament to decide on a new set of international rules governing war, trade, aid, immigration, resource-ownership, environmental policy and so on. Suppose this parliament has 100 members, chosen to reflect the current global population. The regional breakdown of membership is given below. Utilitarians will argue that, although it is unrealistic, this simple thought experiment still has some force. By asking what rules we would get if everyone in the world were represented in global decision-making in this way, we can construct an ideal against which to compare the current international system.

A global utilitarian parliament	
Developing countries in Asia (includes: China 21 and India 17 members, respectively)	59 members
Africa	13 members
Europe	12 members
Latin America and the Caribbean (includes Mexico)	9 members
North America	5 members
Other developed countries (includes Australia, New Zealand, and Japan)	2 members
(Based on United Nations Population Division statistics from 2001.)	

The possibility of extending utilitarianism to the global level also provides a stark new example of both the demandingness objection (from Chapter 5) and the partial compliance problem (from Chapter 6). Suppose I conclude that the utilitarian global parliament would almost certainly implement a programme of radical redistribution, transferring resources from affluent people in the developed world to those in poorer lands. Given the absence of any such strategy in the actual world – and the absence of any global parliament at all – to what extent am I obliged to take up the slack? It is no coincidence that many of those who defend a demanding individual version of utilitarianism also argue for global utilitarianism. (The classic example here is the Australian philosopher Peter Singer.)

The welfare of future people

Unless something goes drastically wrong in the next few centuries, most of the people who will ever live are yet to be born. Our actions have little impact on those who are dead, considerable impact on those currently alive, and potentially enormous impact on those who will live in the future. Perhaps the most significant impact is that our decisions affect who those future people will be, and even whether there will be any future people at all. The threat of environmental crisis gives us some inkling of the magnitude of our impact on future generations. Only in the last few decades have utilitarians really begun to grapple with the complexities of intergenerational ethics. Underlying their often technical debates are some of the deepest moral questions. What makes life worth living? What do we owe to our descendants? How do we balance their needs against our own?

Utilitarian discussion of future people typically begins with a series of puzzles presented by Derek Parfit. Parfit distinguishes two kinds of moral choice. In a *same people choice* our actions affect what will happen in the future, but not who will exist. If our actions do affect who will exist in the future, then we are making a *different people choice*. Utilitarianism treats different people choices the same as same people choices. As we will soon see, this enables it to avoid objections that plague non-utilitarian theories. Unfortunately, utilitarianism faces its own problems regarding the future. Especially difficult are different number choices – where we decide *how many* people ever exist. (The distinction between different number and same number choices – where we determine which people will exist but not how many – is also from Parfit.)

In different number choices, two common interpretations of utilitarianism come apart. These are total utilitarianism (where we seek to maximize the total amount of well-being) and average utilitarianism (maximizing the average level of well-being). The basic argument for total utilitarianism is simple. For any x, if x is valuable, then more x is better than less. The intuition behind average utilitarianism is equally compelling. If we are interested in human well-being, then we want each person to be as happy as possible. Both interpretations can be found in the writings of the classical utilitarians, who did not always distinguish them clearly. This is not normally a problem, because average utilitarianism and total utilitarianism usually coincide. Indeed, in same number choices the outcome with highest average well-being must have highest total well-being – as the average is simply the total divided by the number of people, and all outcomes have the same number of people. In different number choices, however, we can sometimes increase the total while reducing the average. Suppose the only way to increase total well-being is to greatly increase the number of people while greatly reducing their average well-being. In these circumstances total utilitarianism must support population growth. Parfit uses this fact to generate a problem for total utilitarianism.

The repugnant conclusion
For any possible population of at least ten billion people, all with a very high quality of life, there must be some much larger imaginable population whose existence, if other things are equal, would be better, even though its members have lives that are barely worth living.

(Parfit, *Reasons and Persons*, 388)

Suppose we begin with a world where ten billion people all have extremely good lives. Call it A. Imagine a second world (B), where twice as many people are more than half as happy as the people in A. B has more total well-being than A. Now repeat this process until we reach a world where a vast population each have a life that is barely worth living. Call this world Z. As each step increases total well-being, Z must be better than A. Parfit labels this conclusion as "intrinsically repugnant", and argues that utilitarians must avoid it.

The repugnant conclusion has generated a vast philosophical literature. In defence of their theory, utilitarians typically adopt one of two broad strategies. They either restructure their value theory to make A better than Z, or they seek to undermine Parfit's intuition that Z is worse than A. We begin with the second response. When people's intuitions differ, one plausible explanation is that they are really answering different questions. Total utilitarians argue that Parfit confuses a comparison of the values of A and Z with a range of more practical comparisons. Would you rather live in A or Z? Would you choose A over Z? If you were in A, would you be obliged to turn A into Z?

Many philosophers feel that the truly decisive intuition behind the repugnant conclusion concerns actions, not values. If you face a choice between A and Z, then total utilitarianism says you must opt for Z – even if the result is a Z-life rather than an A-life both for yourself and for all your nearest and dearest. If you can create a new species of Z-creature at the cost of greatly reducing the well-being of everyone who already exists, then you ought to do so. Total utilitarianism thus sacrifices all existing people for people who otherwise would not have existed at all. The repugnant conclusion is thus an especially striking example of both the injustice and demandingness objections. Total utilitarianism demands both that you sacrifice yourself and that you sacrifice others. (Imagine a repugnant version of the replicas tale from Chapters 4 and 5, where you can destroy each person and replace them with a large number of much *less* happy clones.)

These demands are very counterintuitive. However, they offer utilitarians a simple solution. Total utilitarianism combines a particular theory of value (the best outcome contains greatest total well-being) with simple consequentialism (you must produce the best outcome). If we are troubled by the demands of total utilitarianism, perhaps we should abandon simple consequentialism. Even if the best outcome is the one with maximum total well-being, individuals are still permitted to favour their own interests. Z is better than A, but you may choose A. (This is an especially appealing strategy if we have already rejected simple consequentialism for other reasons, such as those given in Chapters 6 and 7.) For instance, a rule-utilitarian might argue as follows. Someone who has learnt the best code of rules for the next generation will feel a variety of obligations to specific people, and will be involved in many significant intergenerational projects. In any remotely realistic situation where they face a genuine choice between a world like A and a world like Z, these obligations and commitments will lead such a person to keep their A-world, rather than transforming it into Z.

Some utilitarians are not satisfied with this compromise solution. They think the repugnant conclusion undermines not just simple consequentialism, but also the total utilitarian theory of value. It is not just that we should not aim for Z – we should not even admit that Z is better than A. If we reject total utilitarianism, the simplest alternative is average utilitarianism. It clearly avoids the repugnant conclusion, as A has much higher average well-being than Z.

Before evaluating average utilitarianism, we must deal with an obvious objection. Average utilitarianism seems to tell me to kill everyone whose well-being is below average. This would raise the average level of well-being – and then we would be obliged to kill everyone below the *new* average. Eventually we would have a world with two people, where average utilitarianism tells the happier person to kill the other. To avoid this absurd result, we can simply average over all those who *will ever live*. Killing people with below average lives does not make their lives go away. It makes their lives go worse – thus *lowering* the average level of well-being.

Unfortunately, average utilitarianism faces other objections, which are less easily avoided. In particular, the theory implies that the addition of perfectly isolated, extremely worthwhile lives may make things worse (if average well-being is already high), while the addition of a set of perfectly isolated lives far below the zero level may constitute an improvement (if average well-being is sufficiently low). Parfit illustrates these problems with two tales.

How only France survives
In one possible future everyone's life is well worth living, but climate and cultural traditions give some nations a higher quality of life. The best-off people are the French. In another possible future a new infectious disease makes nearly everyone sterile. French scientists produce just enough of an antidote for everyone in France. All other nations cease to exist.

(Adapted from Parfit, *Reasons and Persons*, 421)

Hell
Most of us have lives which are much worse than nothing. We would kill ourselves if we could, but this is impossible. The people who are torturing us reliably inform us that if we have children, they will make those children suffer slightly less than us – though their lives will still be much worse than not living at all.   (Adapted from Parfit, *Reasons and Persons*, 422)

In each tale, average well-being is higher in the second possible future. So, according to average utilitarianism, we should choose that outcome. Yet Parfit argues that this is absurd. The *mere addition* of lives worth living cannot make things worse, nor can the mere addition of horrible lives make things better.

As with total utilitarianism, one solution is to retain the average utilitarian story about value, but reject simple consequentialism. For instance, a rule-utilitarian might argue that the code of rules that would maximize average well-being in the long run will include specific obligations to other people which would prevent us from making the wrong decision in practice. (For instance, an obligation to do what is best for one's own children would help us avoid the wrong result in the Hell tale.)

Faced with all these puzzles, utilitarians have another option – based on an alternative interpretation of the basic utilitarian ideal. We have been assuming that utilitarianism is indifferent to the identity of persons. Utilitarians seek to maximize levels of well-being across the whole population, without regard for whose well-being is at stake. In particular, total utilitarianism is impartial between *actual people* and *possible people*. It sees no difference between increasing well-being by adding to the well-being of existing people and by adding new happy people. (Average utilitarianism avoids this problem to some extent, but it still counts possible people as well as actual ones when comparing the average well-being of different possible futures.) Many utilitarians – along with most non-utilitarians – reject this degree of impartiality. For these *person-affecting utilitarians*, actual people are more morally significant than possible people. Indeed, possible people do not matter at all – unless they one day become actual. As utilitarians, our goal should be to make people happy, not to make happy people.

Person-affecting utilitarianism avoids the worst versions of the repugnant conclusion. Suppose we are in the A situation. Our world contains 10 billion very happy people. We can greatly increase the population of our world by cloning each person many times. The average quality of life will be greatly reduced by overcrowding, but the total well-being will increase. (Suppose we can escape total ecological disaster by colonizing outer space in such a way that everyone on every planet will have a life barely worth living.) In other words, we can transform our A-world into a Z-world. According to person-affecting utilitarianism, we should *not* change A into Z, as this would be bad for the people who already exist. The fact that the extra people we *could* have created *would* have been happy is not any kind of reason to create them. (Unlike average utilitarianism, person-affecting utilitarianism gives us this result even if the extra people would have been much happier than those who actually exist.)

Unfortunately, person-affecting utilitarianism faces problems of its own, as illustrated by a tale made famous by Parfit. (Parfit's original target is not person-affecting utilitarianism *per se*, but rather the general idea of a person-affecting approach to morality – whether utilitarian or non-utilitarian.)

> **The selfish policy**
> Our community needs energy for an indulgent leisure activity. We choose to
> build a new nuclear power plant in an uninhabited area. We bury the result-
> ing nuclear waste, knowing it will remain radioactive for thousands of years.
> Three centuries later an earthquake releases radiation. Though thousands of
> people are killed by this catastrophe, they all have lives that are worth living.
> (The radiation gives people an incurable disease that kills them at the age of
> 40, but has no other effects.) If we had not built the power plant, patterns
> of migration would have been very different in the intervening years. Have
> we done something wrong?

Under person-affecting utilitarianism, it is hard to fault our decision
in this tale, as we cannot locate any *particular person* who is worse-off
than *they* would have been if we had acted differently. Take a particular
individual (X) killed by the catastrophe. It is almost certain that X's
parents would never even have met if we had not built our plant. So X
herself would never have existed. We thus face a different people choice,
even though our decision is not directly concerned with bringing
people into existence.

Of course, if we had chosen a safer energy policy, then a *different* set of
people would have existed – and *those people* would have been happier
than the actual people actually are. But, as we saw earlier, the whole point
of person-affecting utilitarianism is that the well-being of possible people who never actually exist counts for *nothing*. It thus looks as if, in a
Different People Choice, we can do no wrong. (The one exception is if
we create a new person whose life is *not worth living* – perhaps by using
genetic engineering to create a person with terrible diseases, solely for
medical research purposes. We might say that this person *is* worse-off than
if he had never existed. However, we should note that some philosophers think that even this more modest claim is still incoherent, as it
makes no sense to compare the values of existence and non-existence.)

The challenge for utilitarians is to avoid the repugnant conclusion
without concluding that we can do no wrong in different people
choices. One promising response is to argue that our behaviour should
conform to rules and institutions chosen on the basis of their impact
on actual people. As we saw in Chapter 6, these rules and institutions
will (hopefully) place intuitively plausible limits on our treatment of all
human beings. Gratuitously leaving radioactive material where it will
affect people – or deliberately giving someone a disease – is wrong on
good utilitarian grounds, whether or not the people concerned would
otherwise have existed.

The value of humanity

We have seen that, for utilitarians, the well-being of people in our country is dwarfed by the billions of people who already exist overseas, and the well-being of present people is dwarfed by that of future people. We now bring these two topics together. In the concluding chapter of *Reasons and Persons*, Parfit uses the possibility that human history may be only just beginning to highlight the moral significance of potential catastrophes threatening human survival. We end our discussion of the future of utilitarianism by quoting his remarks, which bring together many of the central themes of this book.

> I believe that if we destroy mankind, as we now could, this outcome would be much worse than most people think. Compare three outcomes:
>
> (1) Peace.
> (2) A nuclear war that kills 99 per cent of the world's existing population.
> (3) A nuclear war that kills 100 per cent.
>
> (2) would be worse than (1), and (3) would be worse than (2). Which is the greater of these two differences? Most people believe that the greater difference is between (1) and (2). I believe that the difference between (2) and (3) is very much greater.
>
> My view is the view of two very different groups of people. Both groups would appeal to the same fact. The Earth will remain inhabitable for at least another two billion years. Civilization began only a few thousand years ago. If we do not destroy mankind, these few thousand years may be only a tiny fraction of the whole of civilized human history. The difference between (2) and (3) may thus be the difference between this tiny fraction and all of the rest of this history. If we compare this possible history to a day, what has occurred so far is only a fraction of a second.
>
> One of the groups who would accept my view are Classical Utilitarians. They would claim, as Sidgwick did, that the destruction of mankind would be by far the greatest of all conceivable crimes. The badness of this crime would lie in the vast reduction of the possible sum of happiness.
>
> Another group would agree, but for very different reasons. These people believe that there is little value in the mere sum

of happiness. For these people, what matters are what Sidgwick called the "ideal goods" – the Sciences, the Arts, and moral progress, or the continued advance towards a wholly just world-wide community. The destruction of mankind would prevent further achievements of these three kinds. This would be extremely bad because what matters most would be the highest achievements of these kinds, and these highest achievements would come in future centuries.

There could clearly be higher achievements in the struggle for a wholly just world-wide community. And there could be higher achievements in all the Arts and Sciences. But the progress could be greatest in what is now the least advanced of these Arts or Sciences. This . . . is Non-Religious Ethics . . . Non-Religious Ethics is at a very early stage. We cannot yet predict whether, as in Mathematics, we will all reach agreement. Since we cannot know how Ethics will develop, it is not irrational to have high hopes.

(Parfit, *Reasons and Persons*, 453–4)

Key points

- Utilitarianism says the most important moral issues are those where the greatest amount of well-being is at stake.
- In the modern world, these issues are global ethics and inter-generational justice.
- A utilitarian global ethic provides a radical critique of existing international practices.
- Most theories of intergenerational justice have difficulty coping with different people choices, and especially with different number choices.
- The three main utilitarian accounts of intergenerational justice are total utilitarianism, average utilitarianism, and person-affecting utilitarianism.
- The key challenges for these three theories are the repugnant conclusion (for total utilitarianism), the mere addition problem (for average utilitarianism), and the non-identity problem (for person-affecting utilitarianism).

Questions for discussion and revision

two Classical utilitarianism

Bentham

1. What is psychological hedonism? How does it differ from ethical hedonism? What role do the two play in Bentham's philosophy?
2. What does Bentham mean by the claim that "Prejudice apart, the game of pushpin is of equal value with the arts and sciences of music and poetry"? Why does he think this?
3. What does Bentham mean by "the greatest happiness of the greatest number"? Why should the legislator adopt this principle? Why does Bentham think the resulting legal system will be superior to the law of his own day?
4. What does Bentham mean by "natural rights"? What does he think of them? Is his view reasonable? Does Bentham mean the same thing by "rights" as we do today?
5. "Punishment causes pain. Pain is bad. Therefore, utilitarians cannot justify punishment." How does Bentham escape this paradox?
6. What is Bentham's panopticon? What does it tell us about his philosophical approach?

Mill

1. What is empiricism? What role does it play in Mill's philosophical system? How does it relate to his support for utilitarianism, for liberalism, for the free market, and for democracy?
2. What is Mill's "proof of utilitarianism" designed to prove? Does the proof contain any hidden or controversial assumptions? Is it a successful proof?

3. Why does Mill need to make a distinction between higher and lower pleasures? What role does the "competent judge" play in his argument? Is the argument successful? Are you a competent judge? Who is?
4. Does Mill's utilitarianism conflict with or reinforce the customary morality of his own day? What about the customary morality of today? (Consider these questions with respect to: justice, liberty, democracy and the status of women.)
5. Why is liberty so important to Mill? Is his general commitment to liberty consistent with his utilitarianism? Is his commitment to free speech consistent with his utilitarianism?
6. What would Mill think about the legalization of drugs in a modern society?

Sidgwick

1. What are the main philosophical differences between Bentham, Mill and Sidgwick? To what extent are these caused by differences in their historical or philosophical situation?
2. What does Sidgwick mean by "intuitionism"? Why does he believe utilitarianism is superior to intuitionism? Are there any methods of ethics other than intuitionism, egoism and utilitarianism?
3. What is Sidgwick's "Dualism of Practical Reason"? Why is it such a problem for his system? What is the best solution to this problem?

three Proofs of utilitarianism

1. What is the theological utilitarian proof of utilitarianism? Would it convince someone who did not believe in God? Would it convince someone who did believe in God?
2. What is Bentham's proof of utilitarianism designed to prove? What are its philosophical presuppositions? Does the proof contain any hidden or controversial assumptions? Are there any salient alternatives that Bentham does not consider? Is his proof successful? (Now answer these same questions for Mill, Sidgwick and Hare.)
3. What is universal prescriptivism? Is it a plausible account of the meaning of moral terms? Does it imply utilitarianism?
4. Why is each of the following characters thought to be a threat to morality: the sceptic, the nihilist, the amoralist, the psychological egoist, the ethical egoist? Do these characters really exist? Are their positions compatible with morality? Does it matter if they are not?
5. What is the method of reflective equilibrium? If you were practising reflective equilibrium, where would you begin? How does this method differ from the intuitionism that both Mill and Sidgwick rejected in the nineteenth century? Is reflective equilibrium compatible with utilitarianism?

four Well-being

1. What do utilitarians mean by *well-being*? Is it the same as *happiness, welfare* or *utility*? Do any of these words mean the same to utilitarians as they do in real life? Is well-being a concept we need if we are to think about morality? (Try to imagine thinking about morality without ever using this concept.)
2. What is *hedonism*? What is *pleasure*? Do these words mean the same to utilitarians as they do in real life? Is pleasure something physiological, something you feel, or something you like? (Or all of these?) Does the plausibility of hedonism depend on how we define pleasure?
3. Is pleasure always good for a person? What about sadistic pleasures? Try to imagine a pleasure that is *intrinsically* bad for the person.
4. Is pleasure the only component of well-being? Or are some pleasures better than others, *for reasons other than intensity of pleasure*? Is it better to be a satisfied pig or a disappointed Socrates?
5. Is it sensible to opt for life in Nozick's experience machine? Is such a life better or worse than life in the real world? Which would you prefer? Which would you recommend to a friend? If you had to choose for your friend, which would you choose?
6. Is it always good (for you) to get what you want? Are there any preferences whose satisfaction does not improve the person's well-being? (Consider the following cases: pointless desires, wanting what is bad for you, self-sacrifice, desires for things beyond the boundaries of your life.)
7. What is the restriction to *I-desires*? Can it save the preference theory?
8. What is the distinction between the *fulfilment* of a desire and its *satisfaction*? Can this distinction save the preference theory?
9. Can the posthumous fulfilment of a desire improve a person's well-being? Does it make their life go better? What does your answer tell you about the plausibility of the preference theory?
10. Suppose you accept that well-being depends entirely on desire-satisfaction. How does the value of a whole human life relate to the satisfaction of individual desires? Do I improve your life if I give you a new desire and then satisfy it? Does the answer depend on the object of the desire? (Compare extending a person's desires via education with making them addicted to a drug.)
11. What is the *objective list* theory of well-being? How does it differ from hedonism and the preference theory? Does it avoid the problems facing those two theories?
12. Which items would you include in a list of the components of well-being? How would you justify each item on your list to someone who rejected it? Is each item good for you even if you do not want it? Is each item good for you even if you do not enjoy it? Does your list reflect your own cultural values or biases? How might you justify it to someone from a very different culture?
13. How do we go from a list of valuable items to the evaluation of whole human lives? Does the best life have more of each valuable item? Must a good life include every item on your list?

14. Which is the best theory of well-being? Why?
15. Is *human* happiness the only value? Is *happiness* the only value? Are there any morally significant differences between humans and other animals? If so, do our three theories of well-being capture and respect those differences?

five Injustice and demands

1. Read through the 14 tales of injustice and unreasonable demands from pages 93–6. Which tale (or tales) do you think poses the most serious threat to utilitarianism? Why? In general, are the injustice tales more or less problematic for utilitarianism than the demandingness tales?
2. (For questions 2 and 3, focus on the tale(s) you selected in question 1.) Why do you think utilitarianism gives the wrong answer in this tale? Does it ignore a crucial morally relevant distinction, or a crucial feature of human persons? If so, which distinction(s) or feature(s)?
3. What would be the most powerful challenge a utilitarian could make to your counter-utilitarian intuitions? How might you defend your intuition? What are the origins of your intuition? Does reflection on those origins undermine your confidence in that particular intuition? Does such reflection undermine your general confidence in your moral intuitions?
4. What is *extremism*? Is it a plausible response to the injustice and demandingness objections to utilitarianism?
5. What is your favourite *non*-utilitarian approach to morality? (This might be a fully developed moral theory, but it need not be.) Does it avoid the injustice and demandingness objections? (Test this by applying your approach to the 14 tales from pages 93–6.) Does your approach have other counterintuitive implications? If so, are these more or less troubling than the problems facing utilitarianism?
6. Consider each of the 14 tales in turn. In each case, how plausible would it be to deny that utilitarianism produces the allegedly counterintuitive result? (For instance, is it plausible to deny that a utilitarian sheriff would hang the innocent person in the first tale?) Can this strategy of denial provide a complete response to the injustice and demandingness objections to utilitarianism?
7. Find one tale where utilitarianism can avoid the allegedly counterintuitive result by rethinking value, and one where it cannot. Now undertake the same task for each specific way of rethinking value: rethinking welfare, rethinking the utilitarian response to welfare, and rethinking distribution.

six Acts, rules and institutions

1. What is *act-utilitarianism*? Is it self-defeating? Is this an objection to act-utilitarianism?

2. What is the distinction between a *criterion of rightness* and a *decision procedure*? Can utilitarians use this distinction to avoid the injustice and demandingness objections?
3. What is *indirect utilitarianism*? How does it differ from act-utilitarianism?
4. Would an indirect utilitarian walk on the grass if no one else was? What if everyone else was? Is indirect utilitarianism *individually* self-defeating? Is it *collectively* self-defeating?
5. Can indirect utilitarianism successfully avoid the injustice and demandingness objections?
6. What is *rule-utilitarianism*? How does it differ from act-utilitarianism, and from indirect utilitarianism?
7. Is rule-utilitarianism guilty of rule worship? Is this an objection to the theory?
8. Can rule-utilitarianism cope with situations of widespread partial compliance?
9. Does rule-utilitarianism collapse into either act-utilitarianism or indirect utilitarianism?
10. Does rule-utilitarianism successfully avoid the injustice and demandingness objections? Whether or not it avoids them completely, does rule-utilitarianism cope with these objections better or worse than indirect utilitarianism?
11. Could rule-utilitarianism help you decide how much money to donate to charity? More generally, could rule-utilitarianism help you to run your own life?
12. What is *institutional utilitarianism*? How does it differ from act-utilitarianism; from indirect utilitarianism; and from rule-utilitarianism?
13. Does institutional utilitarianism successfully avoid the injustice and demandingness objections? Whether or not it avoids them completely, does institutional utilitarianism cope with these objections better or worse than either indirect utilitarianism or rule-utilitarianism?

seven Consequentialism

1. What is *consequentialism*? How is it related to utilitarianism? Can you be a consequentialist without being a utilitarian, and vice versa?
2. Are there any good arguments for consequentialism?
3. What might a non-utilitarian form of consequentialism look like? Is it a plausible theory? Is it more plausible than utilitarian forms of consequentialism?
4. What is *simple consequentialism*? What are its five features? Consider the various forms of utilitarianism presented in Chapter 6. Which of these represent departures from simple consequentialism, and in what ways?
5. What is *satisficing consequentialism*? How does it differ from simple consequentialism?
6. Does satisficing consequentialism successfully avoid the injustice or demandingness objections? Whether or not it avoids them completely, does satisficing consequentialism cope with these objections better or worse than simple consequentialism?

7. What is the distinction between *agent-centred prerogatives* and *agent-centred restrictions*? How does Scheffler incorporate this distinction into his *hybrid view*? How does the hybrid view differ from simple consequentialism? How does it differ from satisficing consequentialism?

8. Does the hybrid view successfully avoid the injustice and demandingness objections? Whether or not it avoids them completely, does the hybrid view cope with these objections better or worse than either simple consequentialism or satisficing consequentialism?

9. What is the difference between *promoting* value and *honouring* value? Which of these two responses to value is more important? Are they both independently morally important, or can one be explained in terms of the other?

10. How does *Kantian ethics* differ from consequentialism? Can Kantian ethics successfully avoid the injustice and demandingness objections? Is Kantian ethics more or less plausible than consequentialism? Discuss with reference to each of the forms of consequentialism discussed in this chapter. (You might also compare Kantian ethics to each of the various forms of utilitarianism presented in Chapter 6.)

11. Are there any other responses to value, distinct from both promoting and honouring? Could a moral theory based on one of these alternative responses successfully avoid the injustice and demandingness objections? Would the resulting theory be more plausible than either Kantian ethics or consequentialism?

12. Were the classical utilitarians (Bentham, Mill, Sidgwick) consequentialists, in the modern sense of the word? What might a non-consequentialist form of utilitarianism look like? Would such a theory be more plausible than consequentialist utilitarianism?

eight Practicality

1. What is the distinction between *actualist* utilitarianism and *probabilistic* utilitarianism? Which is the more plausible form of utilitarianism? Which is easier to apply in practice?

2. Should utilitarianism be based on *objective* or *subjective* probabilities, or on both? Which form of utilitarianism is more plausible? Which is more practical?

3. What are *intrapersonal* comparisons of welfare? Does utilitarianism require such comparisons?

4. What are *interpersonal* comparisons of welfare? Does utilitarianism require such comparisons?

5. What are *cardinal* comparisons of welfare? Does utilitarianism require such comparisons?

6. Recall the three theories of well-being from Chapter 4. Which theory makes it easier for utilitarianism to make *intra*personal comparisons of welfare;

or to make *inter*personal comparisons of welfare; or to make *cardinal* comparisons of welfare? Do your answers affect the judgement you reached in Chapter 4 regarding the comparative plausibility of the three theories?

7. Recall the distinction between act-utilitarianism, indirect utilitarianism, rule-utilitarianism and institutional utilitarianism from Chapter 6. Which evaluations of individual welfare does each of these theories require? Which calculations of consequences does each theory require? Which form of utilitarianism is better placed to make the evaluations and/or calculations it requires? Do your answers affect the judgements you reached in Chapter 6 regarding the comparative plausibility of the four versions of utilitarianism?

8. Does the uncertainty of utilitarian calculations lessen or increase the strength of the utilitarian case for individual freedom, for equality or for democracy? (You might focus on the arguments of J. S. Mill discussed in Chapter 2, or on the arguments of Amartya Sen presented in Chapter 8.)

nine The future of utilitarianism

1. Can utilitarianism provide a stable global ethic? If not, why not? If so, what does that ethic say?

2. Does utilitarianism support global democracy? Is the utilitarian position plausible?

3. What might a global parliament look like? What policies might such a global parliament enact? Would they be good policies? Would they be utilitarian policies?

4. What is the distinction between same people choices and different people choices? Is it morally significant? What is the distinction between same number choices and different number choices? Can utilitarianism cope with different number choices?

5. What is the repugnant conclusion? Is it a problem for utilitarianism? What is the best solution?

6. What is the difference between total and average utilitarianism? When do they coincide? When do they come apart? Which is the better theory?

7. What is person-affecting utilitarianism? Is it better than non-person-affecting utilitarianism? Can person-affecting utilitarianism cope with different people choices?

8. Why does Parfit think that a nuclear war that kills 100 per cent of humanity is much worse than one that kills 99 per cent? Is he correct? Is his position a utilitarian one?

9. Do you share Parfit's optimism about the future of non-religious ethics?

Further reading

General introductions

The best places to start for further material and up-to-the-minute bibliographies are two excellent online encyclopedias: the *Routledge Encyclopedia of Philosophy* and the *Stanford Encyclopedia of Philosophy*. Both are regularly updated, and contain reliable articles on most significant individual philosophers, as well as on most important philosophical topics.

Some good introductions to utilitarianism are Geoffrey Scarre, *Utilitarianism* (London: Routledge, 1996); William H. Shaw, *Contemporary Ethics: Taking Account of Utilitarianism* (Oxford: Blackwell, 1998) and Jonathan Glover, *Utilitarianism and Its Critics* (Englewood Cliffs, NJ: Prentice Hall, 1990).

Good introductions to moral theory in general include Stephen Darwall, *Philosophical Ethics* (Boulder, CO: Westview, 1998); Shelly Kagan, *Normative Ethics* (Boulder, CO: Westview, 1998) and Peter Singer (ed.), *Ethics* (Oxford: Oxford University Press, 2004). Two other books in the Acumen *Understanding Movements in Modern Thought* series are also highly relevant: Tim Chappell, *Understanding Ethics* (forthcoming) and Stan van Hooft, *Understanding Virtue Ethics* (2005).

An accessible, controversial introduction to the utilitarian approach to applied ethics is Peter Singer, *Practical Ethics* (Cambridge: Cambridge University Press, 1993). Robert Goodin's *Utilitarianism as a Public Philosophy* (Cambridge: Cambridge University Press, 1995) presents a contemporary utilitarian approach to political philosophy. For more on political philosophy in general (including a good chapter on utilitarianism), see Will Kymlicka, *Contemporary Political Philosophy* (Oxford: Oxford University Press, 2001).

two Classical utilitarianism

The main primary texts for the authors discussed in Chapter 2 are: William Paley, *The Principles of Moral and Political Philosophy* (1786); William Godwin, *Political Justice* (1793); Jeremy Bentham, *A Fragment on Government* (1776), *An Introduction to the Principles of Morals and Legislation* (1789); J. S. Mill, *System of Logic* (1843), *Principles of Political Economy* (1848), *On Liberty* (1859), *Considerations on Representative Government* (1861), *Utilitarianism* (1861); and Henry Sidgwick, *The Methods of Ethics* (1874). Many of these works are available online – either free on the internet or via your university library. The quotations in the text are from the following editions or sources: Ross Harrison, *Bentham* (London: Routledge, 1983); Peter Singer (ed.), *Ethics* (Oxford: Oxford University Press, 2004); J. S. Mill, *On Liberty* (edited by Gertrude Himmelfarb, Harmondsworth: Penguin Books, 1974); J. S. Mill, *Utilitarianism* (edited by Roger Crisp, Oxford: Oxford University Press, 1998); and Henry Sidgwick, *The Methods of Ethics*, 7th edition (Indianapolis, IN: Hackett, 1981).

Good overviews of classical utilitarianism can be found in Frederick Rosen, *Classical Utilitarianism from Hume to Mill* (London: Routledge, 2003); Scarre, *Utilitarianism*; and Jerome Schneewind, *Sidgwick and Victorian Moral Philosophy* (Oxford: Oxford University Press, 1977). On broader trends in British moral philosophy, see John Skorupski, *English Language Philosophy 1750–1945* (Oxford: Oxford University Press, 1993).

Good overviews of individual philosophers are Ross Harrison, *Bentham*; John Skorupski, *Mill* (London: Routledge, 1991); John Skorupski (ed.), *The Cambridge Companion to Mill* (Cambridge: Cambridge University Press, 1998); Roger Crisp, *Mill on Utilitarianism* (London: Routledge, 1997); Jonathan Riley, *Mill On Liberty* (London: Routledge, 1998) and Schneewind, *Sidgwick and Victorian Moral Philosophy*.

Mill's *Autobiography* (1873) is one of the classic intellectual biographies in the English language, and provides a very candid account of his strange (utilitarian) upbringing. Bart Schultz's *Henry Sidgwick: Eye of the Universe* (Cambridge: Cambridge University Press, 2004) gives a wonderful insight into Sidgwick's life and times, and puts his work in its historical and personal context.

three Proofs of utilitarianism

For literature on the classical utilitarians and their predecessors, see the further reading for classical utilitarianism. (Skorupski's *Mill*, 285–8; and Crisp's *Mill's Utilitarianism*, 67–94 have particularly good discussions of Mill's proof.) G. E. Moore's critique of Sidgwick is in *Principia Ethica* (1903).

R. M. Hare's fullest presentation of his ideas is in *Moral Thinking* (Oxford: Oxford University Press, 1981). D. Seanor and N. Fotion, *Hare and Critics* (Oxford: Oxford University Press, 1988) is an excellent collection of articles discussing various aspects of Hare's moral philosophy.

The classic modern exponent of reflective equilibrium methodology is John Rawls

– see below for references. A very good recent defence from a utilitarian perspective is Brad Hooker, *Ideal Code, Real World* (Oxford: Oxford University Press, 2000), 4–23. For utilitarian critiques of the method, see Peter Singer, "Famine, Affluence and Morality", *Philosophy and Public Affairs*, 1 (1972), 229–43; and Shelly Kagan, *The Limits of Morality* (Oxford: Oxford University Press, 1989), chapter 1.

four Well-being

Good contemporary discussions of well-being are Kagan, *Normative Ethics*, 29–39; and Derek Parfit, *Reasons and Persons* (Oxford: Oxford University Press, 1984), 493–502. Two excellent fuller length treatments, from different perspectives, are James Griffin, *Well-being* (Oxford: Oxford University Press, 1986) and Thomas Hurka, *Perfectionism* (Oxford: Oxford University Press, 1993). For a more empirical approach, see the opening chapters of two books by Partha Dasgupta: *An Inquiry into Well-being and Destitution* (Oxford: Oxford University Press, 1993) and *Human Well-being and the Natural Environment* (Oxford: Oxford University Press, 2001).

Robert Nozick's experience machine tale is found in his *Anarchy, State, and Utopia* (Oxford: Blackwell, 1974), 42–5. Singer's views on animals are presented in *Animal Liberation* (London: Jonathan Cape, 1976) and in *Practical Ethics* (Cambridge: Cambridge University Press, 1993). Sen's defence of a universal desire for freedom is in Chapter 10 of *Development as Freedom* (Oxford: Oxford University Press, 1999).

five Injustice and demands

The ideas behind most of the fourteen tales at the start of the chapter go back to the classical utilitarians and beyond. Two classic discussions of the injustice and demandingness objections are Williams' original presentation of the "integrity" objection in Smart and Williams, *Utilitarianism: For and Against* (Cambridge: Cambridge University Press, 1973) and Peter Singer, "Famine, Affluence and Morality". Rawls' original discussion of the separateness of persons is in *A Theory of Justice* (Oxford: Oxford University Press, 1971), 27. Railton presents his alienation objection in P. Railton, "Alienation, Consequentialism and Morality", *Philosophy and Public Affairs*, 13 (1984), 134–71. For another recent discussion of similar issues, see John Cottingham, "Partiality, Favouritism and Morality", *Philosophical Quarterly*, 36 (1986), 357–73.

The three classic presentations of extremism cited in the text are: Kagan, *The Limits of Morality*; Singer, "Famine, Affluence and Morality"; and Peter Unger, *Living High and Letting Die* (Oxford: Oxford University Press, 1996). For critiques, see Garrett Cullity, "International Aid and the Scope of Kindness", *Ethics*, 105 (1994), 99–127 and Tim Mulgan, *The Demands of Consequentialism* (Oxford: Oxford University Press, 2001), chapter 2.

Parfit's reductionism is developed in *Reasons and Persons*, Part 3. For Brink's view, see "Self-love and Altruism", *Social Philosophy and Policy*, **14** (1997), 122–57. Christine Korsgaard presents a challenge inspired by Kant to the utilitarian account of impartiality in "Personal Identity and the Unity of Agency", *Philosophy and Public Affairs*, **18** (1989), 101–32.

I discuss strategies of denial at greater length in *The Demands of Consequentialism*, chapter 2. For discussions of the evidence regarding the Malthusian argument, see Amartya Sen, *Development as Freedom*, chapter 9. For a rule-utilitarian discussion of the implications of Malthus' argument, see Hooker, *Ideal Code, Real World*, 147–8.

Scanlon's example is from "Contractualism and Utilitarianism" in Sen and Williams (eds), *Utilitarianism and Beyond* (Cambridge: Cambridge University Press, 1982), 103–28. For an introduction to lexicality, see Griffin, *Well-being*, chapter 5. A collection of more complex discussions is Ruth Chang (ed.), *Incom-mensurability, Incomparability and Practical Reason* (Cambridge, MA: Harvard University Press, 1998).

The basic idea of negative utilitarianism has been attributed to Karl Popper. (See James Griffin, "Is Unhappiness More Important Than Happiness?", *Philosophical Quarterly*, **29** (1979), 47–55.) Prioritarianism was introduced into recent philosophical debate by Derek Parfit in "Equality and Priority", *Ratio*, **10** (1997), 202–21.

six Acts, rules and institutions

Griffin's original discussion is in J. Griffin, "The Distinction Between Criterion and Decision Procedure: A Reply to Madison Powers", *Utilitas*, **6** (1994), 177–82. For further discussion of the key distinction between a theory's criterion of rightness and its decision procedure, see Mulgan, *The Demands of Consequentialism*, 37–49.

The most prominent contemporary defender of rule-utilitarianism is Brad Hooker. See especially *Ideal Code, Real World*; and "Rule Consequentialism" in the *Stanford Encyclopedia of Philosophy*. Hooker, Mason and Miller (eds), *Morality, Rules and Consequences* (Edinburgh: Edinburgh University Press, 2000) is a good collection of recent articles on a wide range of issues relating to rule-utilitarianism. For a wide range of objections to rule-utilitarianism, see chapter 3 of Mulgan, *The Demands of Consequentialism*.

A good recent defence of institutional utilitarianism is Goodin, *Utilitarianism as a Public Philosophy*. (See also the works of Amartya Sen cited below.)

The question of whether the classical utilitarians were act-, indirect, rule-, or institutional utilitarians is highly controversial. See the works cited under "classical utilitarianism" above, and especially Rosen, *Classical Utilitarianism from Hume to Mill*; and Crisp, *Mill on Utilitarianism*, especially chapter 5.

seven Consequentialism

Slote presents his satisficing consequentialism in "Satisficing Consequentialism", *Proceedings of the Aristotelian Society*, supp. vol. 58 (1984), 165–76. Scheffler's original presentation of the hybrid view is in his *The Rejection of Consequentialism* (Oxford: Oxford University, 1982). For critique and further literature, see my *The Demands of Consequentialism*, chapters 5 (Slote) and 6 (Scheffler); and *Future People* (Oxford: Oxford University Press, 2006), chapter 4 (Scheffler).

Foot's original trolley example is in "The Problem of Abortion and the Doctrine of Double Effect" reprinted in Fischer and Ravizza (eds), *Ethics: Problems and Principles* (New York: Holt, Rinehart & Winston, 1992), which contains several more recent discussions. For a utilitarian critique of trolley cases, see Unger, *Living High and Letting Die*, chapter 4.

The doing/allowing objection to the hybrid view is presented by Shelly Kagan in "Does Consequentialism Demand Too Much?", *Philosophy and Public Affairs*, 13 (1984), 239–54. Scheffler replies in "Prerogatives without Restrictions", *Philosophical Perspectives*, 6 (1992), 377–97. There is a huge literature on the doing/allowing distinction. One way to get a feel for the debate would be to contrast the approaches of two leading contemporary theorists to the particular distinction between killing and letting die: Francis Kamm (see *Morality, Mortality, Volumes 1 and 2* (Oxford: Oxford University Press, 1994 and 2001)) and Jeff McMahan (see *The Ethics of Killing* (Oxford: Oxford University Press, 2002)).

The terminology of promoting versus honouring is introduced by Philip Pettit. (See "The Consequentialist Perspective" in Baron, Pettit and Slote, *Three Methods of Ethics*, (Oxford: Blackwell, 1997), 92–174. The rest of this book also provides a very good introduction to Kantian ethics and virtue ethics.)

For Kant's most accessible account of moral philosophy, see his *Groundwork of the Metaphysics of Morals*. An excellent historical introduction to contemporary themes in Kantian ethics is Schneewind, "Autonomy, Obligation, and Virtue" in P. Guyer (ed.), *The Cambridge Companion to Kant* (Cambridge: Cambridge University Press, 1992), 309–41. The most famous contemporary theorist inspired by Kant is John Rawls, whose political liberalism owes much to Kant. Samuel Freeman's "John Rawls" in the *Routledge Encyclopedia of Philosophy* is an excellent introduction. Rawls' classic text is *A Theory of Justice*. His most significant later works are *Political Liberalism* (New York: Columbia University Press, 1993) and *The Law of Peoples* (Cambridge, MA: Harvard University Press, 1999). A prominent modern moral theory in a broadly Kantian tradition is T. M. Scanlon's "Contractualism" – see his *What We Owe to Each Other* (Cambridge, MA: Harvard University Press, 1998).

On other responses to value, see Van Hooft, *Understanding Virtue Ethics* in the Acumen *Understanding Movements in Modern Thought* series.

eight Practicality

The most famous exponent of maximin is John Rawls, though he only advocates it in the highly artificial setting of his Original Position. (See Rawls, *A Theory of Justice*, 152–61.) An influential utilitarian critique of the use of maximin even in this limited context is J. Harsanyi, "Can the Maximin Principle Serve as a Basis for Morality?", *American Political Science Review*, 69 (1975), 594–606.

The distinction between ordinal and cardinal rankings is very commonly used in economics, and any good economics textbook will contain reliable technical explanations. Two readable recent applications of related ideas to ethics are John Broome's *Weighing Goods* (Oxford: Oxford University Press, 1991) and *Weighing Lives* (Oxford: Oxford University Press, 2004).

For recent attempts to apply rule-utilitarianism and institutional utilitarianism to the real world, see Hooker, *Ideal Code, Real World*; and Goodin, *Utilitarianism as a Public Philosophy*.

As with most contemporary science, the best place to get further information about the emerging science of positive psychology is via the internet. Two good places to start would be the Centre for Positive Psychology at the University of Pennsylvania and the *Journal of Positive Psychology* (published by Routledge).

For Mill's views on liberty, equality and democracy, see the references above in the section on classical utilitarianism. Sen, *Development as Freedom*, and Dasgupta, *Human Well-being and the Natural Environment* provide extensive references to current debates. A recent excellent summary of the (lack of) available empirical evidence on the comparative merits of majoritarian and constitutional forms of democracy is Ian Shapiro, *The Moral Foundations of Politics* (New Haven, CT: Yale University Press, 2003).

nine The future of utilitarianism

Peter Singer presents his global utilitarianism in *One World* (Melbourne: Text Publishing, 2002). Thomas Pogge offers a similar critique – though not from an explicitly utilitarian angle – in *World Poverty and Human Rights* (Cambridge: Polity, 2002).

The classic text for contemporary discussion of obligations to future generations is Part 4 of Parfit's *Reasons and Persons*, which remains the best place to start. A good recent set of discussions of the repugnant conclusion is Ryberg and Tannsjo (eds), *The Repugnant Conclusion* (Dordrecht: Kluwer, 2004). A prominent current defender of person-affecting utilitarianism is Melinda Roberts (see her "A New Way of Doing the Best We Can", *Ethics*, **112** (2002), 315–50, and *Child versus Childmaker* (Lanham, MD: Rowman & Littlefield, 1998)). For a recent defence of person-affecting intuitions from a non-utilitarian perspective, see Kumar, "Who Can Be Wronged?", *Philosophy and Public Affairs*, **31** (2003), 99–118. For discussion of moderate consequentialist accounts of future generations, especially focusing on rule-utilitarianism, see my *Future People*.

Index